MW00780601

Determining Death
by Neurological Criteria

Current Practice and Ethics

Determining Death
by Neurological Criteria
Current Practice and Ethics

MATTHEW HANLEY

THE NATIONAL CATHOLIC BIOETHICS CENTER
Philadelphia

CATHOLIC UNIVERSITY OF AMERICA PRESS
Washington, DC

Cover design by Nicholas Furton
ISBN 978-0-8132-3318-5

Contents

Foreword

As a practicing neurosurgeon, I am confronted with severely injured patients daily, especially during my trauma on-call duties. Some of the brain injuries in my patients are beyond what modern medicine can heal. Despite heroic efforts by the medical team, the patient progresses to a state commonly referred to as "brain death." Once this clinical diagnosis is made, a series of events is set in motion which will lead to the decision of whether to permit organ donation. At the heart of this decision is the question of whether the patient is indeed dead.

This is a confusing and devastating time for the patient's family and friends. They are told that their loved one has died, but they look up at the sophisticated vital-sign monitors and see that there are still respirations, heartbeat, blood pressure, and good oxygen levels in the blood. The patient looks alive and certainly shares certain characteristics with the living, but they are told that the brain is dead. Legally the patient is dead. But this is more than a medical or legal question. The determination of death by neurological criteria is also a moral question.

The Vatican has long been interested in the morality of determining death by neurological criteria. In service to the Church, Matthew Hanley, who works as a professional researcher, was brought into The National Catholic Bioethics Center as a senior fellow and tasked with examining end-of-life issues, with special emphasis on the determination of death. He has previously written studies on various topics in the areas of public health, philosophy, and theology. His 2009 book, *Affirming Love, Avoiding AIDS: What Africa Can Teach the West*, is a definitive treatment of this crisis and shows that the solution to the spread of sexual disease is not preventive measures, but changes in human behavior.

In *Determining Death by Neurological Criteria: Current Practice and Ethics,* Hanley gives us an erudite and thorough analysis of the topic of brain death. He also expertly discusses death by cardiopulmonary criteria and the general ethics of organ donation (from both living and dead donors). His book encapsulates the governing scientific principles in clear and understandable language for the nonscientist and explains the ethical and philosophical foundations for those who are not philosophers or theologians.

Even though the medical community by and large accepts the neurological criteria for determining death, there are well-formulated and serious arguments in opposition from those in theological and philosophical circles. In response Hanley marshals a wide range of logical and convincing arguments for using the neurological criteria. He often quotes Melissa Moschella, one of the clearest thinkers on this topic. The fundamental metaphysical error in arguments against the neurological criteria, she points out, is the failure to distinguish between internal and external principles of unity. Hanley rightly observes that "no one correctly diagnosed as brain dead has ever regained consciousness," whereas patients have "returned to life" from states of cardiac death and asystole. His conclusion is that death determined by cardiopulmonary criteria is less definitive than that by neurological criteria.

The Catholic Church has never formally addressed the determination of death by circulatory criteria—an interesting omission—which makes the last few chapters of Hanley's book especially intriguing. Hopefully they will serve as a road map for further discussion concerning which of these two standards is definitive for the determination of death.

Determining Death by Neurological Criteria is especially relevant for those in the neurosciences, palliative care, and critical care medicine. After reading this book, doctors, nurses, and all at the bedside will more fully understand the moral reasoning behind the view that a patient diagnosed as brain dead is truly no longer alive. What we see before us is not an integrated human person, but a corpse. The soul has left the body.

I highly recommend this book to those faithful thinkers who oppose the neurological criteria for determining death. Hanley's arguments are so well crafted and supported that I expect some of them will be swayed and rethink their position. The book is also wonderfully resourced, which will provide the interested reader with hundreds of biomedical and philosophical leads for further reading. Finally, as I stated earlier, Hanley writes in a way that is enjoyable to read and easy to comprehend. This book is written for everyone.

Robert J. Buchanan, KM, MD

Robert J. Buchanan, KM, MD, FAANS, is chairman of the Working Group on Consciousness, Neuroscience, and Ethics at the Pontifical Academy for Life. He is the chief of neurosurgery at Ascension Seton Hospitals in Austin, Texas, and an associate professor of neurosurgery, psychiatry, neurology, and psychology at the University of Texas at Austin.

THE CERTAINTY AND UNCERTAINTY OF DEATH

Behind most of man's fears ultimately lurks the fear of death. In his book *Introduction to Christianity*, Joseph Cardinal Ratzinger makes just that point: "In truth—one thing is certain: there exists a night into whose solitude no voice reaches; there is a door through which we can only walk alone—the door of death. In the last analysis all the fear in the world is fear of this loneliness."[1]

Stricken with grave illness in the noon of his days, Hezekiah dreads entering the gates of Sheol, where, as Isaiah tells us, he will never again look on any man (Isa. 38:9–20). Ratzinger highlights that the Old Testament uses only one term, Sheol, for both death and hell: "Death is absolute loneliness. But the loneliness into which love can no longer advance is—hell."[2]

Perhaps the least understood or least contemplated portion of the Apostles' Creed pertains to Christ's

---

1. Joseph Cardinal Ratzinger, *Introduction to Christianity*, 2nd ed. (San Francisco: Ignatius Press, 2004), 301.

2. Ibid.

descent into hell. According to Ratzinger, this event illuminates the consoling truth that "Christ strode through the gate of our final loneliness, that in his Passion he went down into the abyss of our abandonment. Where no voice can reach us any longer, there is he. Hell is thereby overcome, or, to be more accurate, death, which was previously hell, is hell no longer."[3]

Yet even with the hope of eternal life springing from the heart of Christianity, the dreaded prospect of death influences our behavior in ways we cannot or do not want to always recognize. The wages of sin, St. Paul famously wrote, is death (Rom. 6:23). But is this strictly a one-way proposition? The converse also seems to contain a truism of its own: people are subject to slavery through fear of death. The knowledge of death, at least without faith in the gift of eternal life, drives people toward sin. In short, it affects our lives even as we prefer not to think about it.

Plato considered philosophy to be a meditation on death, as have other philosophers down through the ages. Cicero, in fact, felt that "philosophizing is nothing else but consideration of death, *commentatio mortis*."[4] There is even the traditional Western view that "philosophizing is not just meditative consideration of death, but nothing less than learning to die."[5] This, of course,

---

3. Ibid.

4. Cicero, *Tusculanae disputationes* I.75, referenced in Josef Pieper, *Death and Immortality* (South Bend, IN: St. Augustine's Press, 2000), 2.

5. Dominicus Gundissalinus, *De divisione philosophiae*, referenced in Pieper, *Death and Immortality*, 3.

contains an inherent correlative, as Michel de Montaigne observed: "He who would teach men to die would teach them to live."[6] Monks have been known to keep skulls nearby to remind them of their own mortality. This may be one conduit to wisdom, but man, as T. S. Eliot suggested, generally cannot bear too much reality. Most of us do not find thinking of death particularly appealing. We prefer to push it far from our minds even though we know that it is unavoidable.

In his *Confessions*, which are considered to be the first example of existential philosophy, St. Augustine reflects on the unexpected death of a friend during his youth, observing that of all things, only death is certain. (*Incerta omnia, sola mors certa.*)[7] He notes that, at birth, we cannot say with certainty whether any particular event will transpire in one's life or how and to what extent any good or evil will color that life. Certain events and qualities may seem probable for some people in some circumstances, but they never can be guaranteed. Not so with death: "But can you also say of someone: Perhaps he will die, perhaps not? As soon as a man is born, it must at once and necessarily be said: He cannot escape death."[8]

---

6. Michel de Montaigne, "That to Study Philosophy Is to Learn to Die," in *The Complete Works of Montaigne*, trans. Donald M. Frame (Palo Alto, CA: Stanford University Press, 1957), 62, quoted in Pieper, *Death and Immortality*, 3.

7. Augustine, *Enarrationes in psalmos* 39.19, quoted in Pieper, *Death and Immortality*, 9.

8. Augustine, *Commentary on the Psalms*, 38.19, quoted in Pieper, *Death and Immortality*, 9.

That remains as true as ever. But there is some surprising uncertainty—at least some measure of controversy—regarding *when* death takes place, particularly in our own technological era. Nowhere is the controversy more apparent and enduring than in the context of brain death.

Historically, the utter and sustained lack of heartbeat and breathing sufficed in determining that someone had died. In times past, if a person sustained a neurologic injury (brain damage) severe enough to result in apnea (the loss of the capacity to breathe) the result invariably was a rapidly diminishing content of oxygen in the blood and subsequent cardiac arrest.[9]

The advent of the mechanical ventilator changed all that. Circulation could be sustained through artificially maintained respiration. In certain situations, modern technology is thus capable of nothing short of halting the physiological mechanism by which death naturally occurs.

Patients in modern intensive care units (ICUs) are now routinely maintained by means that were previously unimaginable. Incidentally, the application of positive-pressure ventilation to patients with severe, otherwise fatal neurological injuries was an unanticipated

---

9. James L. Bernat, "The Whole-Brain Concept of Death Remains Optimum Public Policy," *Journal of Law, Medicine and Ethics* 34.1 (Spring 2006): 35–43, doi: 10.1111/j.1748 -720X.2006.00006.x.

development discovered by the anesthesiologist Björn Ibsen during the polio epidemic of 1952–1953.[10]

This intervention has enabled many vulnerable patients to achieve remarkable recoveries. But for those patients who suffered complete and irreversible brain damage, it led to an entirely new and unanticipated condition: an irreversible and apneic coma. This is a state beyond a mere coma, which pioneering French scientists in the 1950s termed *coma dépassé*.

This condition soon became known colloquially as brain death. Some think the term is unfortunate because it may imply the death of an organ only rather than of the individual. Its fundamental clinical manifestations are irreversible coma, apnea, and brain stem areflexia. Each of these cardinal features must be present. Typically, brain death results from massive trauma to the brain, a massive stroke, or the lack of oxygenated blood following cardiopulmonary arrest (global hypoxic-ischemic neuronal damage).

For the first time in history, human beings had to come to terms with an unsettling phenomenon: the patient who by virtue of total and irreversible loss of brain function, is unable to move, breathe, and react— and thereby appears dead—but who, by virtue of the mechanically maintained circulation, also exhibits characteristics associated with the living. The question

---

10. Michael Souter and Gail Van Norman, "Ethical Controversies at End of Life after Traumatic Brain Injury: Defining Death and Organ Donation," *Critical Care Medicine* 38.9 suppl (September 2010): S502–S509, doi: 10.1097 /CCM.0b013e3181ec5354.

had to be answered, were these unfortunate patients in fact alive or dead?[11]

Establishing the Validity of Brain Death

In 1957, a year before the term *coma dépassé* came into use and a decade before the Harvard Ad Hoc Committee first proposed a set of neurological criteria for determining death, Pope Pius XII maintained that it falls on the doctor, the competent medical authority, "to give a clear and precise definition of 'death' and the 'moment of death' of a patient who passes away in a state of unconsciousness."[12] The very most the Church could do was reiterate the conditions that make it legitimate to accept the better judgment of those who are competent to determine the moment of death.

The Pope's statement recognizes that the language of the Church and the language of medicine do not seamlessly align when it comes to understanding and describing death. The Church conceives of death as the separation of body and soul. Modern medicine does not think in terms of the soul, which no laboratory test can detect. It uses other units of measurement, concepts, and terminologies such as the irreversible cessation of the functioning of the organism as a whole. The task is to determine when these conceptions of death overlap. Addressing this area

---

11. Bernat, "Whole-Brain Concept of Death," 14–28.

12. Pius XII, "The Prolongation of Life: An Address to an International Congress of Anesthesiologists—November 24, 1957," *National Catholic Bioethics Quarterly* 9.2 (Summer 2009): 330.

of potential conflict, Pope St. John Paul II stressed that "the Church does not make technical decisions" about such matters. Nonetheless, she can assimilate the evidence that medical science supplies in light of "the Christian understanding of the unity of the person."[13]

Over several decades, the Church has closely followed the scientific and philosophical deliberations pertaining to brain death and has consistently accepted that total brain death constitutes the death of the human person. In 2006, when the Pontifical Academy of Sciences last discussed the topic, its summary was plainly titled "Why the Concept of Brain Death Is Valid as a Definition of Death."[14] The Vatican's acceptance of brain death reflects the recognition that the medical profession overwhelmingly endorses it as equivalent to death, its reasons for doing so have solid physiological grounding, and importantly, the concept of whole-brain death seems compatible with a sound anthropology.

Although the Church eventually explicitly accepted brain death, early critics validly observed that the assertion that brain death amounts to human death, which

13. John Paul II, Address to the Eighteenth International Congress of the Transplantation Society (August 29, 2000), n. 5.

14. John Haas has explained the Church's approach to the issue in considerable detail: "Thus three times now, under two different pontificates, the Pontifical Academy of Sciences has concluded that the neurological criteria are a legitimate basis for determining death." John M. Haas, "Catholic Teaching regarding the Legitimacy of Neurological Criteria for the Determination of Death," *National Catholic Bioethics Quarterly* 11.2 (Summer 2011): 287.

as we shall see later on, is ultimately a physiologically precise assertion, was not supported by a robust philosophical argument.[15]

In their carefully reasoned 1979 book *Life and Death with Liberty and Justice*, Germain Grisez and and Joseph Boyle are justifiably critical of the Harvard committee in this respect: "Even if it is correct to maintain—as we shall argue—that an individual whose entire brain is dead is no longer a living person, the Harvard committee's approach seems to have involved a method in principle unacceptable: A private group here consciously attempted to effect the legal nonpersonhood of a class of individuals."[16]

A few short years later, however, a robust and influential bio-philosophical rationale emerged.[17] It held

---

15. "A Definition of Irreversible Coma: Report of the Ad Hoc Committee of the Harvard Medical School to Examine the Definitions of Brain Death," *JAMA* 205.6 (August 5, 1968): 337–340, doi: 10.1001/jama.1968.03140320031009.

16. Germain Grisez and Joseph M. Boyle, *Life and Death with Liberty and Justice: A Contribution to the Euthanasia Debate* (Notre Dame, IN: University of Notre Dame Press, 1979), 66.

17. James L. Bernat, Charles M. Culver, and Bernard Gert, "On the Definition and Criterion of Death," *Annals of Internal Medicine* 94.3 (March 1981): 389–394, doi: 10.7326/0003-4819-94-3-389. See also President's Commission for the Study of Ethical Problems in Medicine and Biomedical and Behavioral Research, *Defining Death: A Report on the Medical, Legal and Ethical Issues in the Determination of Death* (Washington, DC: The Commission, 1981), available at https://repository.library.georgetown

that brain death necessarily involves the cessation of the integrative functioning of the organism as a whole, reflecting our greater and more precise physiological understanding of the mechanism of death. In the modern technological era, the inability to maintain cardiopulmonary function no longer necessarily signifies death. Similarly, remarkable and indubitable as that development is, artificially sustained cardiopulmonary function no longer necessarily signifies life.

It takes nothing away from valid criticisms of the Harvard committee to acknowledge that the essential clinical elements it identified as necessary for the diagnosis of brain death—known cause of coma, apnea, and unresponsiveness—have remained constant. The criteria have, in fact, been validated by their reliability: no one who has ever been properly diagnosed as dead by the neurological criteria has ever recovered.

Problematic Relationship with Organ Transplantation

A lot hinges on the determination of which physiological functions signify life. Most fundamentally, of course, is the overarching and universally binding consideration that we should not treat the living as if they are dead and vice versa. Determining the status of such patients also has pressing practical and ethical implications regarding

---

.edu; and "Guidelines for the Determination of Death: Report of the Medical Consultants on the Diagnosis of Death to the President's Commission for the Study of Ethical Problems in Medicine and Biomedical and Behavioral Research," *JAMA* 246.19 (November 13, 1981): 2184–2186, doi: 10.1001/jama.1981.03320190042025.

organ donation and transplantation. In particular, it is essential to establish with moral certainty when a person has died, because it is not licit to harvest unpaired vital organs from a living person. The extraction of organs must not cause or hasten the death of imminently dying donors. This is the premise of the ethical standard known as the dead donor rule, the linchpin of the entire organ transplantation enterprise.

Prominent figures representing prestigious institutions have made disturbing proposals to abandon such a rule for the explicitly utilitarian goal of obtaining more organs. They maintain that brain death is a "useful fiction."[18] It does not amount to human death, but organ retrieval from those subjects is nonetheless justified. If that view were to be accepted, persons who are not dead could become eligible to "donate" their vital organs. Even from a pragmatic point of view, veering away from strict adherence to this principle runs the risk of seriously jeopardizing public trust.

Although the Church recognizes the good that can come from organ transplantation, it rejects outright any utilitarian justification for redefining death. There has been no more robust opponent to the prevailing utilitarian mindset than the Catholic Church. *Veritatis splendor* condemns utilitarianism in the most unequivocal terms. In 2008, Pope Benedict XVI clearly insisted that vital organs can be extracted only *ex cadavere* and reiterated that "the principal criteria of respect for the life of the donator must always prevail so that the

---

18. Robert D. Truog and Franklin G. Miller, "'Brain Death' Is a Useful Fiction," *Critical Care Medicine* 40.4 (April 2012): 1393–1394, doi: 10.1097/CCM.0b013e3182451a08.

extraction of organs be performed only in the case of his/her true death."[19]

In 1989, John Paul II acknowledged both the needs of the sick for whom transplantation may be their best hope and the difficulty of arriving at a definition of death that all would find acceptable. He also clearly highlighted the moral line that may not be crossed:

> It is conceivable that in order to escape certain and imminent death a patient may need to receive an organ which could be provided by another patient, who may be lying next to him in hospital, but about whose death there still remains some doubt. Consequently, in the process there arises the danger of terminating a human life, of definitively disrupting the psychosomatic unity of a person. More precisely, there is a real possibility that the life whose continuation is made unsustainable by the removal of a vital organ may be that of a living person, whereas the respect due to human life absolutely prohibits the direct and positive sacrifice of that life, even though it may be for the benefit of another human being who might be felt to be entitled to preference.[20]

The dead donor rule is, in essence, the only means by which this tension may be resolved, the only mechanism by which the retrieval of vital organs may proceed with the consent of the donor to offer part of his or her own self as a gift for the benefit of another.

---

19. Benedict XVI, Address to participants at an international congress organized by the Pontifical Academy for Life (November 7, 2008).

20. John Paul II, Address to the working group on the determination of brain death and its relationship to human death (December 14, 1989), n. 5.

From the beginning, critics recognized the dangers of a utilitarian interpretation of brain death and objected not only to the concept, but also to the process by which it was originally sanctioned. Some felt that the neurological criteria for determining death essentially amounted to a convenient redefinition of death for the sake of two other goals: procuring organs for transplantation and protecting physicians from legal action after withdrawing ventilator support. These two factors, it must be said, were explicitly invoked in the rather skeletal statement produced by the Harvard committee. That the committee explicitly entertained these motives is alone sufficient to provoke a measure of suspicion. The various motivations of any one individual or institution, however, do not have a direct bearing on the validity of the diagnosis.

The manner in which the concept of brain death was introduced and initially justified certainly left much to be desired. It seems indisputable that utilitarian arguments accompanied the presentation of the neurological criteria.[21] However, while some have continued to portray brain death inaccurately as a mere construct in the service of organ transplantation, "most importantly, the confirmation of brain death allows the withdrawal of therapies that can no longer conceivably benefit an individual who has died."[22]

---

21. For a critique of brain death, including the utilitarian elements of the Harvard Committee statement, see D. Scott Henderson, *Death and Donation: Rethinking Brain Death as a Means for Procuring Transplantable Organs* (Eugene, OR: Pickwick Publications, 2011).

22. M. Smith, "Brain Death: Time for an International Consensus," *British Journal of Anaesthesia* 108 suppl. 1 (January 2012): i6, doi: 10.1093/bja/aer355.

Moreover, although brain death and organ transplantation rose to prominence around the same time and have become inextricably linked since the late 1960s, they evolved independently. Brain death is an effect of advances in intensive care, whereas organ transplantation is a result of advances in surgery and immunosuppressive therapies. The authors of a historical review of these parallel medical developments speculate that if other sources of transplantable organs become available in the future, for example, from advances in stem cell techniques, the determination of brain death and the practice of transplantation will become disassociated.[23]

A Poorly Understood Phenomenon

The fact of the matter is that brain death is a challenging phenomenon to absorb. On top of its complexity and gravity, there is also a deep undercurrent of sensitivity emblematic of any issue in contemporary bioethics, which by its very nature is "a moral theology of crises."[24] Brain death has achieved a degree of consensus atypical of many other contentious bioethics issues,

---

23. Calixto Machado et al., "The Concept of Brain Death Did Not Evolve to Benefit Organ Transplants," *Journal of Medical Ethics* 33.4 (April 2007): 197–200, doi: 10.1136/jme.2006.016931.

24. Nicanor Pier Giorgio Austriaco, *Biomedicine and Beatitude: An Introduction to Catholic Bioethics* (Washington, DC: Catholic University of America Press, 2011), 5. "In other words, it is a branch of moral theology that responds to scenarios where an individual is confronted by a particular life crisis."

but it remains "one of the oldest and most enduring problems in bioethics and biophilosophy."[25]

Relatively few people die in the ICU as a result of traumatic brain injury. Most die in the "normal" way, as persons have since time immemorial. Consequently, it is not surprising that the vast majority of people identify death with the cessation of cardiac function, whereas a fairly small minority, perhaps instinctively, associate it with the total and irreversible loss of brain functioning.[26]

Most people confronted with the news that a loved one is "brain-dead" have probably never considered what that means or even that the determination of death could be a source of controversy. Many may suppose that since other vital systems still function, albeit only through technological intervention, only the brain has died.

It is not uncommon for family members to express the belief that their loved one *really* died when the ventilator was removed. One 2004 survey found that although 98 percent of respondents had heard of brain death, only 33.7 percent believed that brain-dead bodies are actually

25. James L. Bernat, "How the Distinction between 'Irreversible' and 'Permanent' Illuminates Circulatory-Respiratory Death Determination," *Journal of Medicine and Philosophy* 35.3 (June 2010): 242, doi: 10.1093/jmp /jhq018.

26. Michael, G. Hennerici, "Surviving Areas of Brain Tissue in Brain Death: Is the Whole More Than the Sum of Its Parts?," in *The Signs of Death: Proceedings of the Working Group 11–12 September 2006*, ed. H. E. Msgr. Marcelo Sánchez Sorondo (Vatican City: Pontifical Academy of Sciences, 2007), 101–113.

dead.[27] A 2003 study by the same lead investigator reached an even more dramatic finding: about 60 percent of family members suspected their loved one was still alive after being informed of the brain death diagnosis.[28]

Books with titles such as *Twice Dead* and scholarly debates published with the opposing titles "You Only Die Twice" and "You Only Die Once" reflect a measure of the lingering confusion and disagreement over what constitutes death. Yet an obvious truism must stand, as James Bernat has pointed out: "All organisms must be either alive or dead; none can be both or neither."[29] Dead and alive "are fundamental underlying states of an organism, whereas dying and disintegration are processes that happen to that organism: dying while the organism is alive and disintegration when the organism

---

27. Laura A, Siminoff, Christopher Burant, and Stuart J. Younger, "Death and Organ Procurement: Public Beliefs and Attitudes," *Social Science and Medicine* 59.11 (December 2004): 2330, doi: 10.1016/j.socscimed.2004.03.029, referenced in Eun-Kyoung Choi et al., "Brain Death Revisited: The Case for a National Standard," *Journal of Law, Medicine and Ethics* 36.4 (Winter 2008): 831, doi: 10.1111/j.1748-720X.2008.00340.x.

28. Laura Siminoff, Mary Beth Mercer, and Robert Arnold, "Families' Understanding of Brain Death," *Progress in Transplantation* 13.3 (September 2003): 222, doi: 10.1177/152692480301300309.

29. James L. Bernat, "The Biophilosophical Basis of Whole-Brain Death," *Social Philosophy and Policy* 19.2 (July 2002): 331, doi: 10.1017/S0265052502192132.

is dead."[30] Nevertheless, it is common to hear that people declared dead by the neurological criteria are being kept alive on life support. That is a mischaracterization. A more appropriate term would be, as some practitioners note, "organ preservation support."

To suppose otherwise is to fail to grasp one of the central features of brain death: it is a *retrospective* determination. Death has already occurred by the time the battery of clinical tests are completed and all the criteria are satisfied. The clinical examination does not and cannot, of course, specify precisely when death occurred.

---

30. James L. Bernat, "A Defense of the Whole-Brain Concept of Death," *Hastings Center Report* 28.2 (March–April 1998): 15.

2

THE NEUROLOGICAL
CRITERIA FOR DEATH

Brain death has been an established diagnosis for decades, but it nonetheless remains rather poorly understood by the public and even by health professionals. It has achieved a high degree of consensus that is remarkably rare among other contested bioethics topics even as dissent and controversy have persisted in some quarters for decades. Today, opposition to the concept of brain death is largely confined to the realm of philosophy.

A thorough protocol has been established for determining brain death, beginning with a preliminary neurological evaluation and culminating with a clinical examination. These elements, taken together, constitute the "neurological criteria" for determining death. They are also frequently called the "clinical criteria," since brain death is determined primarily on the basis of the clinical examination. These criteria are based on the widely accepted guidelines that the American Academy of Neurology (AAN) developed in 1995 and updated in 2010. If a patient fails to satisfy all of the clinical criteria, death should not be pronounced.

Prerequisites and Confounders

Not everyone with a severe brain injury undergoes a clinical examination for brain death. Certain prerequisites must be met, and confounders must be ruled out before a clinical examination is conducted. This is a very important part of the process. When a misdiagnosed case of brain death surfaces in the media, it frequently involves the failure to account for an underlying factor that should have precluded an attempt to assess brain stem viability.

Clinicians must be able to establish the proximate cause of a patient's coma and that it is irreversible. This is typically accomplished through a combination of patient history, neuroimaging, examination, and laboratory tests. The presence of drugs that affect the central nervous system must be ruled out, typically by examining patient history and conducting drug screening. If such drugs are present, sufficient time must elapse for them to be cleared out of the system. Accounting for the presence of narcotics has taken on additional prominence in light of the surging opioid epidemic.

A patient who has been treated with hypothermia following a heart attack should also not be immediately be evaluated for brain death. Patients with acidosis, electrolyte imbalance, or endocrine disturbances likewise should not be evaluated. The presence of neuromuscular blocking agents—ascertained by maximal ulnar nerve stimulation—also should preclude a clinician from progressing further toward a possible death determination. Normal core temperature and systolic blood pressure must be achieved before proceeding to a clinical examination. Only once all these conditions are satisfied should a clinical examination take place to determine if the patient exhibits the core characteristics of brain death: total lack of responsiveness (coma), total absence of brain stem reflexes, and apnea.

Clinical Examination

The coma is confirmed by observing the lack of response to noxious stimuli, particularly no eye opening or movement. The remaining core part of the clinical examination comprises a battery of tests that seek to elicit reflexes mediated by the brain stem: Does the pupil in either eye react when exposed to a bright light? Is there any eyelid movement when the cornea is touched by tissue paper, water, or a cotton swab? Is there any eye movement when the head is briskly rotated vertically and horizontally or when each external auditory canal is irrigated with cold water? Is there any facial muscle movement or grimacing when the patient is exposed to noxious stimulus or when intense pressure is applied in particularly sensitive locations such as the supraorbital ridge? Does the patient exhibit pharyngeal (gag) or tracheal (cough) reflexes?

A single manifestation of any of these reflexes would rule out a diagnosis of brain death, since anyone with a functioning brain stem will automatically react to such stimulation. Once these functions are lost, however, no treatment can restore them. This is why the medical authorities find brain death convincing.

Clinicians are to follow specific, detailed meth-odologies when conducting each of these tests, since particular complications could lead to an erroneous interpretation. In addition, there are cases in which one or more tests are not feasible. For instance, a clinician would not briskly rotate the head of a patient presenting with a spinal injury. Similarly, some clinical tests may be difficult to conduct reliably if the patient presents with severe facial trauma.

The final portion of the clinical examination is the apnea test, which assesses the patient's capacity to breathe. This is obviously very important, since patients who are capable of breathing on their own are not dead. The patient must satisfy several prerequisites before the apnea test is conducted. These principally pertain to core temperature and systolic blood pressure, but any underlying condition resulting in chronic retention of carbon dioxide also needs to be taken into consideration. Clinicians must also prepare for this test by preoxygenating the patient.

An important feature of the apnea test is the "carbon dioxide challenge." When the respiratory center in the medulla oblongata (at the base of the brain stem) detects sufficiently high levels of carbon dioxide in the blood, it triggers the impulse to inhale.[1] To test the involuntary contraction and relaxation of the respiratory muscles, clinicians should induce hypercarbia, an abnormally high level of carbon dioxide in the blood, because the

---

1. See President's Council on Bioethics, *Controversies in the Determination of Death: A White Paper by the President's Council on Bioethics* (Washington, DC: PCBE, 2008), 22–27.

goal is to verify total brain stem destruction.[2] If the brain stem is functioning, inducing hypercarbia will result in respiration.

Simply disconnecting a patient from the ventilator is "potentially concerning" because it does not "induce maximal stimulation of the respiratory centres."[3] It is not uncommon for some patients to experience abnormally *low* levels of carbon dioxide in the blood (hypocarbia) after being treated with hyperventilation to alleviate increased intracranial pressure. Disconnecting such a patient from a ventilator for ten minutes could very well result in apnea even though carbon dioxide levels are not high enough to ensure a lack of response from the brain stem. Some practitioners have been apprehensive about complications that could arise from conducting an apnea test, such as hypoxemia, hypotension, and cardiac arrhythmias.[4] As a result, they prematurely end the test or even avoid it altogether.

---

2. Eelco F. M. Wijdicks, "The Clinical Criteria of Brain Death throughout the World: Why Has It Come to This?," *Canadian Journal of Anesthesia* 53.6 (June 2006): 540–543, doi: 10.1007/BF0302184.

3. Ibid., 540.

4. Sudhir Datar et al., "Completing the Apnea Test: Decline in Complications," *Neurocritical Care* 21.3 (December 2014): 392, doi: 10.1007/s12028-014-9958-y. "The apnea test is a crucial component of the clinical diagnosis of brain death. Apprehension about hypoxemia, hypotension, and/or cardiac arrhythmias may sometimes lead clinicians to avoid performing or prematurely terminate the apnea test. The purpose of this

Not all methods of apnea testing are the same. The provision of oxygen before and during the apnea test is an important variable in the apnea testing process. In a detailed retrospective chart review evaluating the safety of this oxygenation–diffusion method of apnea testing, researchers found the approach to be "very safe, provided appropriate prerequisites are met."[5] In fact, it led to a major decrease in the number of unattempted or terminated apnea tests compared with a previous series of cases that did not use this technique. Subsequent research similarly supports the prevailing view that this method of apnea testing is safe.[6]

The AAN is careful to specify that its guidelines for the clinical examination and for ancillary tests are not evidence-based but are intended as a practical tool for clinicians. They are grounded in current understanding of physiology, accumulated observation and practice, and reasoned judgment. They are intentionally conservative. If a person meets all of the criteria for brain death, it is reasonable to conclude that he does differ profoundly from patients who are clearly alive but suffer from severe neurological impairment.

---

study was to perform a contemporary re-evaluation of the safety of the apnea test."

5. Ibid.

6. Ali Daneshmand, Alejandro A. Rabinstein, and Eelco F. M. Wijdicks, "The Apnea Test in Brain Death Determination Using Oxygen Diffusion Methods Remains Safe," *Neurology* 92.8 (February 19, 2019): 386–387, doi: 10.1212/WNL.0000000000006963.

Brain death is a distinct diagnosis, and testing protocols need to be approached with absolute rigor. It is also important if somewhat complicating to note that some clinical observations are compatible with the diagnosis of brain death, including normal blood pressure, the absence of diabetes insipidus, and even some spontaneous movements not mediated by the brain. Given such complexities, discerning brain death accurately naturally requires corresponding expertise.

Ancillary Tests

If the apnea test or any other brain-stem reflex test cannot be satisfactorily completed, ancillary tests may also be conducted. If the result of the clinical examination is unclear, the clinician may prudently choose to forgo making a determination of death altogether. Alternatively, he may judge that ancillary tests could offer additional evidence to resolve ambiguities associated with the initial clinical exam.

These tests mainly detect electrical activity and blood flow in the brain. The currently validated, preferred tests are the electroencephalogram (EEG), cerebral angiogram, and nuclear scan. These tests cannot override clinical findings or independently establish brain death. The clinician especially needs to be on guard for false positives: cases in which the ancillary test indicates brain death even when the patient does not actually meet the clinical criteria. (Sometimes these tests are performed before the first or second clinical examination.) Consequently, the AAN cautions that if the clinical presentation is unreliable, physicians should refrain from declaring death.

Some would prefer greater reliance on ancillary testing because the clinical examination is subject to human error. While the desire for maximum confidence in the determination is easy to appreciate, ancillary tests also require human interpretation and can result in error as well. Therefore, they supply no grounds for reversing the prevailing view that ancillary tests should be subordinate and connected to the clinical examination.

Ancillary tests remain optional in most countries and are confined mainly to particular circumstances.[7] Ancillary tests are not required in the Unites States,[8] but they tend to be used more commonly in Europe. According to a 2015 study of 1,844 cases at forty-two intensive care units in Spain, just 5 percent of cases were determined utilizing the clinical examination alone.[9]

---

7. M. Smith, "Brain Death: Time for an International Consensus," *British Journal of Anaesthesia* 108 suppl 1 (January 2012): i8, doi: 10.1093/bja/aer355.

8. David M. Greer and Gioacchino G. Curiale, "End-of-Life and Brain Death in Acute Coma and Disorders of Consciousness," *Seminars in Neurology* 33.2 (April 2013): 157–166. The authors note that some "techniques such as CT angiography, magnetic resonance angiography, and SSEPs are not validated and should not be used." Conventional four-vessel angiography remains the gold standard, although it is "limited by its invasiveness, time and resource intensiveness, and lack of guidelines for its interpretation" (162). The AAN has also supported the use of other techniques such as the EEG and transcranial Doppler.

9. D. Escudero et al., "Intensive Care Practices in Brain Death Diagnosis and Organ Donation," *Anaesthesia* 70.10 (October 2015): 1130, doi: 10.1111/anae.13065.

At present there remains no single, universally applicable ancillary test. In confirming brain death, these tests take two general forms: they either confirm the loss of bioelectrical activity in the brain or establish cerebral circulatory arrest. One of the oldest and simplest tests, the EEG, is challenging to interpret and may not be interpretable in as many as 20 percent of cases.[10] It is susceptible to error in both directions: a false declaration of death or a false declaration that death has not occurred. With respect to the blood flow tests, none are validated to diagnose brain death. Likewise, no laboratory blood test is at present able to confirm brain death.[11]

In the process of developing its 2010 guidelines, the AAN evaluated the battery of available tests and plainly concluded that "there is insufficient evidence to determine if newer ancillary tests accurately confirm the cessation of function of the entire brain."[12] Efforts are ongoing to systematically assess the accuracy of ancillary tests compared with the recognized reference standards: clinical diagnosis, four-vessel angiography,

10. Patricia D. Scripko and David M. Greer, "An Update on Brain Death Criteria: A Simple Algorithm with Complex Questions," *Neurologist* 17.5 (September 2011): 239, doi: 10.1097/NRL.0b013e318224edfa.

11. Katharina M. Busl and David M. Greer, "Pitfalls in the Diagnosis of Brain Death," *Neurocritical Care* 11.2 (October 2009): 276–287, doi: 10.1007/s12028-009-9231-y.

12. Eelco F. M. Wijdicks et al., "Evidence-Based Guideline Update: Determining Brain Death in Adults—Report of the Quality Standards Subcommittee of the American Academy of Neurology," *Neurology* 74.23 (June 2010): 1914, doi: 10.1212/WNL.0b013e3181e242a8.

and radionuclide imaging.[13] It is hoped that a higher-quality evidence base will emerge to aid clinicians in the selection of ancillary tests.

Recent research sheds light on how ancillary tests can return false positives. One study highlighted three cases in which transcranial Doppler ultrasound indicated that brain death had occurred; subsequent clinical examination, however, contradicted those findings.[14] These patients had a skull defect or extraventricular drain, which apparently affects the accuracy of the test, although it is not clear why. Even outside this context, where the test may well be of use, physicians must use caution when interpreting it, especially considering that it returns no signal at all (which could lead to a false positive) in 5 to 10 percent of cases.[15]

But misdiagnoses can run both ways. For example, cerebral perfusion is necessary for life. Yet our understanding of the differing etiologies and mechanisms by which the brain dies now enables us to make a rather remarkable observation: although the absence

---

13. Michaël Chassé et al., "Ancillary Testing for Diagnosis of Brain Death: A Protocol for a Systematic Review and Meta-analysis," *Systematic Reviews* 2.100 (November 9, 2013), 100, doi: 10.1186/2046-4053-2-100.

14. Bradford B. Thompson et al., "The Use of Transcranial Doppler Ultrasound in Confirming Brain Death in the Setting of Skull Defects and Extraventricular Drains," *Neurocritical Care* 21.3 (December 2014): 534–538, doi: 10.1007/s12028-014-9979-6.

15. Scripko and Greer, "Update on Brain Death," 239.

of cerebral blood flow is a reliable indicator of death, a person may be dead even with a measure of cerebral blood flow.[16]

There are a couple reasons for this. In some cases, "there is an intrinsic pathology affecting the brain's neurons on a cellular level," which despite sufficient cerebral blood flow, can result in brain death. In addition, intracranial swelling can be a primary cause of brain death, but it is not necessarily "an indefinite phenomenon." Once swelling gradually subsides, intracranial pressure may decrease and cerebral blood flow may return even after irreversible damage has already been done. This suggests that "there may be a time-sensitive nature to the examinations using [cerebral blood flow] as a marker of brain death."[17] It is therefore possible for this type of test to inaccurately imply that death has not occurred.[18]

These considerations should help resolve the concerns held by some ethicists that a clinical exam is insufficient. Nevertheless, the suggestion that blood flow tests should be required everywhere may be a good idea. In some cases, confounding factors may make a clinical examination difficult or impossible. Requiring ancillary tests might result in greater vigilance, as James Bernat has noted.

---

16. Manraj K.S. Heran, Navraj S. Heran, and Sam D. Shemie, "A Review of Ancillary Tests in Evaluating Brain Death," *Canadian Journal of Neurological Sciences* 35.4 (September 2008): 413, doi: 10.1017/S0317167100009069.

17. Ibid., 414.

18. Scripko and Greer, "Update on Brain Death," 239.

Although the public and the medical community should insist on a high standard, clinical guidelines must acknowledge that technological imaging tests cannot independently verify whether a patient is brain-dead.[19] Furthermore, existing evidence has led the AAN, in essence, to caution "against the use of new technologies before proper validation."[20]

With these limitations in mind, it seems reasonable to conclude that patients who unequivocally fulfill the clinical criteria for brain death are dead even if, as critics stress, they do not meet the requirement of the complete loss of *all* brain activity. In short, the overall evidence base for ancillary tests confirms the contention held by most authorities that brain death is primarily a clinical diagnosis. The best possible ancillary tests should be used when appropriate to corroborate, clarify, or assist in the evaluation.

Whole-Brain Death

Whole-brain death is by far the most accepted formulation worldwide. But what is meant by the term *whole*-brain death and similar locutions such as *all*-brain function? On the one hand, this terminology is meant to specify that all the regions of the brain must be accounted for and to distinguish brain death from severe brain injury, particularly those limited to the "higher" regions of the brain. On the other hand, the

19. David Y. Hwang, Emily J. Gilmore, and David M. Greer, "Assessment of Brain Death in the Neurocritical Care Unit," *Neurosurgery Clinics of North America* 24.3 (July 2013): 469–482, doi: 10.1016/j.nec.2013.02.003.

20. Scripko and Greer, "Update on Brain Death," 237.

absolutist implication of such terminology could con-
note the requirement that every single neuron or sign of
activity in the brain must be irreversibly absent.

The former interpretation clearly seems to reflect how
the terminology developed organically. The requirement
that every neuron be destroyed simply is not necessary
for a reliable diagnosis.[21] Whole-brain death—or as the
President's Council on Bioethics has termed it, "total
brain failure"—refers to the irreversible loss of the brain's
critical functions. It specifies that the "basic" functions
of the brain stem and the "higher" functions of the cerebral cortex must be irreversibly lost. This signifies that
the brain as a whole no longer functions. It depicts an
underlying reality and cannot be taken in a strictly literal
sense. As Nicanor Austriaco observes, "One can *never*
clinically diagnose the total loss of brain function."[22]

Whole-brain death is, in that sense, "an approxi-
mation and therefore may be potentially misleading,"
as Bernat has granted. Although virtually all neurons
may be destroyed in many cases, the clinical examination cannot ensure that small nests of brain cells are
not present.[23] In this context some ambiguity could be
introduced: "It is difficult to state the maximum number

---

21. A. Battro et al., "Why the Concept of Brain Death
Is Valid as a Definition of Death," in *The Signs of Death:
Proceedings of the Working Group 11–12 September 2006*,
ed. H. E. Msgr. Marcelo Sánchez Sorondo (Vatican City:
Pontifical Academy of Sciences, 2007), xxvii.

22. Nicanor Austriaco, "Is the Brain-Dead Patient *Really*
Dead?," *Studia Moralia* 41.2 (2003): 299, original emphasis.

23. James L. Bernat, "How Much of the Brain Must Die in
Brain Death?," *Journal of Clinical Ethics* 3.1 (Spring 1992): 24.

and location of brain neurons that can survive despite the presence of clinically diagnosed brain death."[24] Elsewhere, Bernat specifies that while a few neurons may function in isolation, whole-brain death "requires that a *critical* number of neurons permanently cease functioning, namely, those that subserve the essential activities of the hemispheres, diencephalon, and brain stem."[25]

A certain discrepancy, as some have stressed, does linger inasmuch as persistent neuroendocrine regulation is not compatible with the neurological criteria in countries with whole-brain death laws.[26] For instance, pituitary function may remain relatively normal in patients fitting the whole-brain death profile.[27]

In some cases of confirmed brain death, surviving hypothalamic neurons are capable of secreting the hormone vasopressin, thereby preventing the onset of diabetes insipidus. In light of such facts a measure of

---

24. Ibid., 25.

25. James L. Bernat, "Brain Death: Occurs Only with Destruction of the Cerebral Hemispheres and the Brain Stem," *JAMA Neurology* 49.5 (May 1992): 569, original emphasis, doi: 10.1001/archneur.1992.00530290161027. "Because these isolated nests of independently operating neurons no longer contribute critically to the functions of the organism as a whole, their continued activity remains consistent with the whole-brain criterion of death."

26. Michael Nair-Collins, Jesse Northrup, and James Olcese, "Hypothalamic-Pituitary Function in Brain Death: A Review," *Journal of Intensive Care Medicine* 31.1 (January 2016): 47, doi: 10.1177/0885066614527410.

27. D. J. Powner et al., "Hormonal Changes in Brain Dead Patients," *Critical Care Medicine* 18.7 (July 1990): 702–708.

interpretation is needed, which is to say a certain meaning must be attributed to the ongoing function. Bernat concludes that in the context of clearly established brain death, any remaining neuronal activity does not constitute a critical feature of a living organism, because "these isolated nests of neurons no longer contribute to the functioning of the organism as a whole; their functioning is now irrelevant to the dead organism, just as is the continued functioning of its liver cells."[28]

A clinical examination cannot possibly determine the status of every neuron in the brain. It can, however, assess whether the capacity to facilitate the overall integration of the organism is present. This helps explain why brain death is compatible with a sound anthropology.

Higher-Brain Formulation

Advocates of the "higher-brain," or neocortical, formulation maintain that a functioning brain stem cannot be the decisive indicator that a person is alive. Instead, they claim it is the higher portion of the brain that matters because that is where cognition, identity, and memory are located. Once this region is destroyed and those rational capacities no longer can be manifested, the person has died.

This would mean that a wide range of patients, including those in a persistent vegetative state (PVS), could be considered dead despite the retention of spontaneous respiratory activity, a clear sign that the brain stem is still functioning. Robert Veatch, one of the leading proponents of the higher-brain standard, has

---

28. Bernat, "How Much of the Brain Must Die," 25.

proposed that death should not be strictly correlated with a biological phenomenon but rather defined as "the irreversible loss of that which is essentially significant to the nature of humans."[29]

An insurmountable problem with this view (aside from overlooking spontaneous breathing) is that Veatch identifies the ability to interact socially and the capacity for "experience" as essential aspects of human life. This moves death into the subjective realm, where profound disability may permissibly and arbitrarily override biological reality.[30] Although this radical conception has not been enacted into law anywhere, it remains a recurring theme in the bioethics literature. The philosopher John Lizza, for instance, maintains that persons who have lost all mental functions are dead even if they can breathe on their own, because they have lost what he terms

---

29. Robert M. Veatch, *Transplantation Ethics* (Washington, DC: Georgetown University Press, 2000), 87. Eberl accuses Veatch of equating "the end of a human person's biological existence" with "the loss of 'the capacity to think, feel, be conscious and aware of other people.'" Jason T. Eberl, "A Thomistic Understanding of Human Death," *Bioethics* 19.1 (February 2005): 34, doi: 10.1111/j.1467 -8519.2005.00423.x, citing Robert M. Veatch, "Whole-Brain, Neocortical, and Higher Brain Related Concepts," in *Philosophy and Medicine*, vol. 31, *Death: Beyond Whole-Brain Criteria*, ed. Richard M. Zaner (New York: Springer, 1988), 173.

30. For a detailed analysis, see Larry Hostetter, "Higher-Brain Death: A Critique," *National Catholic Bioethics Quarterly* 7.3 (Autumn 2007): 499–504.

"psychophysical integration."[31] Similarly, the authors of a 2014 article take the extreme position that

> The ontological state of permanently vegetative patients is unclear: such patients are neither straightforwardly alive nor simply dead. ... Some relatives and experts believe it is right for patients to be shifted from their currently unclear ontological state to that of being straightforwardly dead, but many are concerned or even horrified by the only legally sanctioned method guaranteed to achieve this, namely withdrawal of clinically assisted nutrition and hydration. A way of addressing this distress would be to allow active euthanasia for these patients. This is highly controversial; but we argue that standard objections to allowing active euthanasia for this particular class of permanently vegetative patients are weakened by these patients' distinctive ontological status.[32]

In one survey of neurologists in the United States, most respondents indicated that the loss of higher-brain functions is the primary justification for brain death.[33] Perhaps this troubling finding reflects a lack of formation

31. John P. Lizza, "Defining Death: Beyond Biology," *Diametros* 55 (March 2018): 1–19, doi: 10.13153/diam.1172.

32. Stephen Holland, Celia Kitzinger, and Jenny Kitzinger, "Death, Treatment Decisions and the Permanent Vegetative State: Evidence from Families and Experts," *Medicine, Health Care and Philosophy* 17.3 (August 2014): 413, doi: 10.1007/s11019-013-9540-y.

33. Ari R. Joffe et al., "A Survey of American Neurologists about Brain Death: Understanding the Conceptual Basis and Diagnostic Tests for Brain Death," *Annals of Intensive Care* 2 (2012), 4, doi: 10.1186/2110-5820-2-4.

or merely personal opinion, but it is not consistent with prevailing medical understanding and the law. The extent to which such views translate into actual practice is unknown, but they add to the urgency of discovering how accurately brain death is determined in practice.

Unfortunately, important distinctions between particular conditions are not always presented accurately in the media or grasped clearly by the public. In particular, there appears to be a good deal of public confusion regarding the difference between brain death and PVS. Some commentators conclude that patients in a vegetative state are more or less like brain-dead bodies and vice versa. Both may have extensive higher-brain damage, but they are distinguished by the presence or absence of total brain destruction.

The tragic case of Terri Schiavo, which became a national flashpoint in the culture wars, is a case in point. She suffered severe neurological injury but was not brain-dead. She was breathing on her own. She was alive in a PVS. But since she had only a remote prospect of recovering her cognitive capabilities, some felt it was justifiable to withdraw all remaining forms of support, including nutrition and hydration. Others erroneously lumped her into the category of the dead.

The fact that autonomous vegetative operations persist in patients with profound neurological damage but not in bodies with clear indications of brain death actually makes a reliably accurate diagnosis more challenging. Some patients are obviously alive and have a surprising degree of awareness, which has gone undetected until only quite recently: "Whereas the diagnosis of death based on neurological criteria can be made with a high degree of certainty, based on clinical criteria and, in some cases, with the use of ancillary means such as neuroimaging, the same cannot be said about the so-called vegetative state, which I prefer to call chronic neurological unresponsiveness."[34]

Whole-brain death is not common. The probability that a comatose adult patient is brain-dead is rather low, typically because anoxic injuries usually do not progress to the point of destroying the brain stem. Leading neurologists estimate that this probably occurs in less than 5 percent of cases.[35]

Brain-Stem Formulation

The United Kingdom uses a brain-stem formulation, which, as the name implies, requires only the destruction of the brain stem and makes no explicit requirement that the higher brain also be destroyed.[36] The clinical criteria for the whole-brain and the brain-stem formulations of death, however, are essentially identical in that the bedside examination assesses activity that is mediated by the brain stem. Yet however unlikely, there remains a possibility that a person whose brain stem is destroyed but who nonetheless retains some higher-brain functions could be declared dead in the United Kingdom but not in the United States.

---

34. José C. Masdeu, "Neuroimaging: A Window into Total Brain Destruction and the Unresponsive States," in Sorondo, *Signs of Death*, 229.

35. Eelco F. M. Wijdicks et al., "There Is No Reversible Brain Death," *Critical Care Medicine* 39.9 (September 2011): 2205, doi: 10.1097/CCM.0b013e318222724e.

36. The United Kingdom is the most notable example, but other countries, such as India, have followed suit.

This remains largely theoretical, and no cases have been reported. There are, however, "unusual but existing cases of catastrophic brainstem lesion (often of haemorrhagic origin) that spared the thalami and cerebral cortex." Using a brain-stem formulation, a patient in this condition "can be declared brain dead in the absence of clinical brainstem function, despite intact intracranial circulation."[37] This scenario, however, would be "exceedingly rare" and would involve a "massive brainstem infarct or haemorrhage that destroys the midbrain, pons and medulla but spares the cerebral hemispheres."[38]

The rarity of such cases does not obviate the discrepancy between the two formulations even if the difference is "less than it first appears."[39] On the contrary, it reinforces the conclusion that only the whole-brain formulation provides a "fail-safe mechanism to eliminate false-positive brain death determinations and assure the loss of the critical functions of the organism as a whole."[40] Indeed, many recognize the need for consensus

---

37. Steven Laureys, "Death, Unconsciousness and the Brain," *Nature Reviews Neuroscience* 6.11 (November 2005): 901.

38. James L. Bernat, "Controversies in Defining and Determining Death in Critical Care," *Nature Reviews Neurology* 9.3 (March 2013): 166.

39. D. Gardiner et al., "International Perspective on the Diagnosis of Death," *British Journal of Anaesthesia* 108 suppl 1 (January 2012): i25, doi: 10.1093/bja/aer397.

40. James L. Bernat, "The Whole-Brain Concept of Death Remains Optimum Public Policy," *Journal of Law, Medicine and Ethics* 34.1 (Spring 2006): 39, doi: 10.1111/j.1748 -720X.2006.00006.x.

and standardization to offset current inconsistencies and variability in both policy and practice. In all likelihood, the United Kingdom would therefore have to reconsider its adherence to the brain-stem formulation.[41]

There is a clear difference between the partial devastation of the brain and the total death of the brain even though whole-brain death has "never meant that literally *all* brain activity must cease."[42] Determining brain death remains principally a clinical diagnosis, a condition verified by examination at the bedside. This, of course, assumes that all preconditions are satisfied and confounding factors are ruled out. It is not mainly a determination made by recourse to laboratory tests and sophisticated technological detection. Sometimes, if the clinical examination is inconclusive or cannot be thoroughly performed, ancillary tests can be helpful. Nevertheless, death is evident to the trained physician at the bedside by virtue of its external manifestations.

---

41. M. Smith, "Brain Death," i6–i9.

42. George Khushf, "A Matter of Respect: A Defense of the Dead Donor Rule and of a 'Whole-Brain' Criterion for Determination of Death," *Journal of Medicine and Philosophy* 35.3 (June 2010): 357 note 3, original emphasis, doi: 10.1093/jmp/jhq023.

3

Inconsistent Application of the Neurological Criteria

Existing institutional guidelines provide the most substantive and representative picture of how rigorously and consistently the neurological criteria are applied. Although this currently is the most accurate method of measuring compliance, it has two major limitations: First, it does not measure the actual adherence of practitioners. Second, some institutional guidelines lack sufficient rigor such that even if they were always properly followed, critically injured patients still could wrongly be declared dead.

The inconsistencies observed at the institutional level are attributable in part to considerable latitude in federal law. The Uniform Determination of Death Act does not specify a universally applicable methodology or series of tests to determine death. Instead, it establishes a general standard that death occurs either when circulatory and respiratory functions have irreversibly ceased or when all functions of the brain, including in the brain stem, have ceased. The act states that the "determination of death must be made in accordance with accepted medical standards," but it largely leaves this up to the discretion of the competent authorities—physicians—in each given case.[1]

Allowing a certain leeway may have its merits, since clinical practice evolves, particularly in response to new technologies. However, the current lack of uniformity, having developed organically over time, may fuel a measure of public suspicion that the neurological criteria may sometimes be less than objective. It is also noteworthy that the approach in the United States differs fundamentally from that in other countries, which mandate specific tests and procedures.

In 2008, Eun-Kyoung Choi and colleagues called for a national medical and legal standard for determining brain death. Taken together, the lack of standardized procedures and the variability of institutional guidelines, particularly in light of visible and sometimes aggressive efforts to procure organs, tend to "reduce the credibility of brain death determination and may contribute to public concerns that physicians are using brain death to hasten patients' death determination solely for the purpose of organ donation."[2] The authors

---

1. Jesse Barber et al., "Guidelines for the Determination of Death: Report of the Medical Consultants on the Diagnosis of Death to the President's Commission for the Study of Ethical Problems in Medicine and Biomedical and Behavioral Research," *JAMA* 246.19 (November 13, 1981): 2184, doi: 10.1001/jama.1981.03320190042025.

2. Eun-Kyoung Choi et al., "Brain Death Revisited: The Case for a National Standard," *Journal of Law, Medicine and Ethics* 36.4 (Winter 2008): 831, doi: 10.1111/j.1748 -720X.2008.00340.x.

maintain that sufficient expert consensus exists to make a federal policy on brain death feasible even amidst the present impediments to its establishment.

The national standard they envision would take into account the inconsistencies that have emerged between the law, which stipulates the cessation of all functions of the entire brain, and the actual clinical determination of death, which is compatible with some detectable brain activity. The standard would clarify that a certain level of brain activity, such as neuroendocrine or thermoregulatory function, does not invalidate a determination of death when the essential criteria have been fulfilled.[3]

The authors argue that the AAN guidelines are well suited to serve as a basic model for a national standard. They also conclude that such a standard necessitates some mechanism of enforcement that reliably and routinely evaluates clinical practice. After all, as other commentators have subsequently observed, "strong evidence-based guidelines do not always lead to consistent practice."[4]

In the absence of a national standard, states are left to devise their own laws concerning the determination of death. In 2002, Eelco Wijdicks reported on the differing legal requirements within the United States:

> The US states have comparable statutes but differences are notable. Virginia specifically calls for a specialist in the neurosciences. Florida mandates

---

3. Ibid., 828.

4. Richard P. Lee, "Brain Death: There Can Be No Doubt!," *Critical Care and Resuscitation* 13.4 (December 2011): 216.

two physicians; one must be the treating physician, and the other must be a board-eligible or board-certified neurologist, neurosurgeon, internist, pediatrician, surgeon, or anesthesiologist. In addition, New York and New Jersey have changed their statutes to accommodate religious objections. These amendments require physicians to honor these requests and to continue medical care despite evidence of loss of brain function. One physician determination is sufficient in most states, but statutes in California, Alabama, Iowa, Louisiana, Florida, Virginia, Kentucky, and Connecticut require independent confirmation by another physician. In Alaska and Georgia, a registered nurse is delegated authority to declare death according to the statutory criteria, but with subsequent certification by a physician within 24 hours. In Virginia, there is limited authority given to a registered nurse.[5]

Hospital Guidelines

The lack of a national standard, combined with the leeway afforded by the law, has obliged institutions to develop their own protocols. Therefore, actual medical practice potentially varies from one institution to the next. This in turn leaves open the possibility that a patient could be declared dead at one hospital but not another.

Since the existing guidelines are not identical, it is crucial that every protocol complies with the core, essential requirements for determining brain death. Institutions, for instance, may have different requirements with

---

5. Eelco F. M. Wijdicks, "Brain Death Worldwide: Accepted Fact But No Global Consensus in Diagnostic Criteria," *Neurology* 58.1 (January 8, 2002): 21.

respect to the number or type of professionals who must examine a patient before a determination of death can be made. That type of variation may not be desirable, but in itself it is not necessarily cause for alarm, particularly considering that different institutions have different resources and specialties. James Bernat, for instance, is not necessarily troubled by the fact that neurologists are not always required to make the determination: "I'm more concerned that whoever is performing these evaluations is doing it correctly. In many hospitals the examinations are done by intensivists, and they know what they're doing; I wouldn't discount them one bit. And I've seen residents do a more thorough job than the attending neurologist because they tend to be more cautious and have been trained to do it correctly."[6] This is not to minimize the importance of qualified and experienced physicians. On the contrary, one retrospective study found that when experienced examiners follow established guidelines, the determination of death is highly reliable.[7]

David Greer and colleagues concur that every institutional guideline does not have to be identical, but they make an important precautionary distinction that "certain key elements such as the prerequisites for testing, the details of the clinical examination, and the details of the apnea testing should be uniformly agreed upon

6. James L. Bernat, quoted in Kurt Samson, "Top Hospitals Routinely Disregard Brain Death Guidelines, Study Finds," *Neurology Today* 7.21 (November 6, 2007): 14, doi: 10.1097/01.NT.0000298559.26531.c9.

7. Choi et al., "Brain Death Revisited," 833.

on a national level, and deviations from these principles not be taken lightly."[8]

Several studies have documented the different methods hospitals endorse to determine brain death. In 2004, David Powner and colleagues at the University of Texas, sufficiently concerned that actual practice does not adhere to existing standards, surveyed six hundred randomly selected hospitals to compare the individual institutional policies against the guidelines developed in 1995 by the American Academy of Neurology (AAN). Only 106 policies were ultimately included in the final analysis. Even in this relatively small sample, considerable variability among the policies was observed. Importantly, 12 percent of the hospitals "did not identify any precautionary factors or strategies to avoid invalid testing."[9] Only 42 percent of the policies specified that the physician responsible for determining death be excluded from the subsequent act of organ retrieval and transplantation, a troubling breach of the elementary ethical norm to maintain a clear separation of roles.

Ninety-six percent of hospitals did require apnea testing, which sounds reassuring. Yet the fact that such an

---

8. David M. Greer et al., "Variability of Brain Death Determination Guidelines in Leading US Neurological Institutions," reply to Tia Powell et al., *Neurology* 71.22 (November 25, 2008): 1839–1840, doi: 10.1212/01.wnl.0000339381.23073.11.

9. David J. Powner, Michael Hernandez, and Terry E. Rives, "Variability among Hospital Policies for Determining Brain Death in Adults," *Critical Care Medicine* 32.6 (June 2004): 1285, doi: 10.1097/01.CCM.0000127265.62431.0D.

essential diagnostic procedure is not universally stipulated is cause for concern. Furthermore, 37 percent did not specify what level of $PaCO_2$ safely confirms apnea, and "only three hospitals defined the level of hypoxemia to be induced when a patient might be insensitive to hypercarbia."[10] In other words, hospitals did not always specify the sufficient threshold for ensuring maximal stimulation of the respiratory centers in the brain stem. The authors, in short, uncovered undesirable diversity and concluded that "the possibility of an erroneous diagnosis of death, therefore, is of concern."[11]

A few years later, a team of specialists assessed the extent of variation between guidelines from the top fifty neurological institutions and the 1995 AAN guidelines. These more robust results were published in 2008 in *Neurology*. Three of the forty-one responding institutions did not have any specific guidelines.[12] All thirty-eight submitted guidelines were analyzed by five discrete categories: guideline performance, preclinical testing, the clinical examination, apnea testing, and ancillary tests. Despite some areas of consistency, the survey found "striking and unexpected areas of discrepancy."

There was marked variation in the types of physicians permitted to conduct the exam, the number of exams required, and the interval between exams. For

---

10. Ibid., 1287.

11. Ibid., 1285.

12. David M. Greer et al., "Variability of Brain Death Determination Guidelines in Leading US Neurologic Institutions," *Neurology* 70.4 (January 22, 2008): 284–289, doi: 10.1212/01.wnl.0000296278.59487.c2.

instance, 71 percent of the guidelines required multiple exams, and 44 percent further specified that two different physicians perform the exams. The waiting interval between exams ranged from one to twenty-four hours, with the most common interval being six hours. There was also ambiguity regarding the precise age at which a patient should be considered an adult, which is important because extra precautions are needed for the pediatric population.

The vast majority of guidelines included the prerequisites for a clinical exam in general terms, but there was wide variation between specific prerequisites and the AAN guidelines. Of particular concern was the surprising absence in many guidelines of a requirement to establish an underlying cause of brain death or to rule out the presence of sedatives and paralytics, acid-based disorders, and endocrine disorders. It was uncommon for all three of these confounding factors to be mentioned in the same institutional guideline.

It might be considered encouraging that 89 percent mentioned hypothermia as a confounding factor, but eleven different minimum temperatures were provided to measure it. Similarly, ruling out drug intoxication was a common feature of the guidelines, but specific drugs varied widely. Likewise, absence of shock was mentioned in over 70 percent of the guidelines, but shock was defined in widely varying terms. Furthermore, 24 percent of the guidelines did not specify an acceptable blood pressure.

The portions of the guidelines pertaining to the clinical examination contained the greatest degree of consistency, but they were not without troubling deviations. Among the most prominent was the fact that only 87 percent specified that the patient should exhibit no spontaneous respirations. Compliance with several other specific brain-mediated reflexes was also far from uniform. The presence of coma, however, was universally mandated, and apnea testing was required in all but one of the guidelines.

Although apnea testing was almost universally required, variation in the techniques used to assess it surfaced as an area of concern, particularly since this component of the evaluation has the greatest potential for misinterpretation. Only 66 percent of the guidelines required the measurement of arterial blood gas composition prior to testing, and only 39 percent specified a normal $PaCO_2$ level. An apnea test administered under these conditions might fail to maximally stimulate the respiratory centers, preventing an accurate assessment.

There also were inconsistencies in the method of pre-oxygenation, the use of supplemental oxygen during the test, and patients' body temperature at time of testing. The issue of repeating the test if it was inconclusive or stopping the test in progress because of instability also deviated from AAN guidelines.

Finally, the role of ancillary testing was established inconsistently. For instance, 34 percent of the guidelines did not specify the situations in which ancillary tests are recommended or helpful. The most common ancillary tests were mentioned frequently, but specific aspects of performing them were not. These details are important because ancillary tests can be performed incorrectly or misinterpreted. The researchers also note that potentially promising ancillary techniques are included in institutional guidelines, but many of these are not validated and are of "questionable value in comparison" to the gold standard of conventional angiography.

Despite the positive findings in this survey, the authors also described the results as "disturbing." In fact, their findings, alongside ample other indications of practice variability, suggest that "the accuracy of assessment for brain death across institutions, and even among individual physicians, may be drawn into question." An editorial in the *British Journal of Anaesthesia* would later deem it "surprising, and of some significant concern, that deviation from this practice guideline is relatively widespread."[13]

Bernat endorsed these findings as "extremely valid." The bottom line, he maintained, is that "despite standards and accepted tests for brain death decisions, many hospitals and individuals involved in these decisions are not doing it right. It's disturbing."[14] These are, after all, well-regarded institutions that specialize in neurology. At present, Bernat notes, it is up to the hospital clinical review boards to ensure that practice guidelines are fully incorporated into hospital policy. In his view, the most consequential discrepancies in need of standardization include accounting for confounders, administering apnea tests, and conducting anatomical brain examinations.

---

13. M. Smith, "Brain Death: Time for an International Consensus," *British Journal Anaesthesia* 108 suppl 1 (January 2012): i7, doi: 10.1093/bja/aer355.

14. Bernat, quoted in Samson, "Top Hospitals Routinely Disregard Brain Death Guidelines," 13–14.

In a major 2013 article updating the status of current practice, Bernat wrote that this survey "disclosed a shocking lack of standardization, despite availability of the accepted AAN guidelines for over a decade. In one institution, apnoea testing, which has been a prerequisite in every published battery of brain death tests since the 1970s, was, inexplicably, not required. ... The need for greater uniformity in performing and recording the tests is obvious."[15] It is not sufficient that such occurrences are rare, considering the repugnance of any misdiagnosis. As Powner emphatically maintains, "An infallible conclusion is mandatory. ... Clinical practice must not be permitted to become careless, abbreviated, or casual."[16] Greer and colleagues, in fact, ended their 2008 *Neurology* article by suggesting that the 1995 AAN guidelines be updated, particularly to rectify areas in which variability of practice is extensive.

Guideline Variability Since 2010

On the basis of these findings, the AAN did update its practice parameters in 2010.[17] There has been some positive response to these revisions. For instance, in 2011

---

15. James L. Bernat, "Controversies in Defining and Determining Death in Critical Care," *Nature Reviews Neurology* 9 (March 2013): 167–168, doi: 10.1038/nrneurol .2013.12.

16. David J. Powner, "Certification of Brain Death: Take Care," *Lancet* 373.9675 (May 9–15, 2009): 1587, 1588, doi: 10.1016/S0140-6736(09)60887-4.

17. Eelco F. M. Wijdicks et al., "Evidence-Based Guideline Update: Determining Brain Death in Adults—Report of the Quality Standards Subcommittee of the American

the state of New York revised its 2005 brain death guidelines to be in greater conformity with the 2010 AAN parameters.[18] Individual hospitals within New York, however, are not bound by law to follow these guidelines. Incidentally, the 2005 guidelines were developed following a survey of brain death policies that found extensive and significant variability between institutions as well as "deviations from accepted guidelines."[19]

The principle change was reducing the number of clinical brain stem examinations from two to one. Other components of the evaluation process have also been updated, including the role of the waiting period. The 2005 guidelines recommended an "arbitrary" interval of six hours between the first and second examination. In the current iteration, no specific amount of time is proscribed, but physicians are required to rule out the recovery of brain function before proceeding with the single clinical examination. The apnea test is the final piece: if apnea is present, death is declared.[20]

In 2016, Greer and colleagues published an evaluation of institutional compliance with the 2010 AAN

Academy of Neurology," *Neurology* 74.23 (June 8, 2010): 1911–1918, doi: 10.1212/WNL.0b013e3181e242a8.

18. New York State Department of Health and New York State Task Force on Life and the Law, "Guidelines for Determining Brain Death," November 2011, http://www.health.ny.gov/.

19. Tia Powell, James Zisfein, and John Halperin, "Variability of Brain Death Determination Guidelines in Leading US Neurologic Institutions," comment on Greer et al., 1839.

20. Department of Health and Task Force on Life and the Law, "Guidelines for Determining Brain Death," 2.

guidelines. This representative survey of 492 hospitals composing, 80 to 85 percent of facilities in the United States where a determination of death can be made, provides us with the most up-to-date and comprehensive assessment of institutional approaches to determining brain death.[21] The 2010 practice parameters were designed to be conservative, and they are clear, simple, and straightforward. For that reason, the research team anticipated that hospitals would have conformed their policies accordingly. Protocols pertaining to adult patients were evaluated in five broad categories: who is designated to perform the examination, the necessary prerequisites, the particular aspects of the clinical examination, the details of apnea testing, and the approaches to ancillary testing. The researchers identified significant variability across all five of these categories despite the fact that institutions have by and large incorporated the main aspects of the AAN parameters.

Overall, the authors were concerned that less experienced junior physicians are still empowered by some policies to make the determination of death, and that there is considerable inconsistency regarding the number of required examinations as well as the prescribed waiting periods in between examinations. They also found compliance to be lagging. In particular, physicians do not consistently rule out confounding factors, conduct thorough apnea tests, or establish the absence of lower-brain-stem function. They also found that many protocols do not include details of approved ancillary

---

21. David M. Greer et al., "Variability of Brain Death Policies in the United States," *JAMA Neurology* 73.2 (February 2016): 213–218, doi: 10.1001/jamaneurol.2015.3943.

tests—for example, how to perform them—and that some ancillary tests are included before they are validated and approved.

They speculated that the 2010 AAN parameters have not been adopted more uniformly, in part because no brain-dead body has regained brain function after a determination of death was made in full compliance with the 1995 standards. This may lead to a certain complacency or false reassurance that no modifications are necessary. In any event, without sufficient internal or external motivation to maximize vigilance, thorough compliance with the latest guidelines can fail to become a priority.

Greer and colleagues' overarching conclusions are corroborated by a more targeted study that sought to directly compare the policies of the top fifty neurologic institutions in the United States in 2015 with the policies of the top fifty institutions in 2006.[22] Published in early 2017, these results provide another perspective from which to gauge how much uniformity has improved over time. Forty-nine institutions provided policies for analysis, 76 percent of which had been established or revised after the AAN guidelines were updated in 2010. The authors were disappointed that 16 percent of the policies dated from before 2010. (Ten percent did not specify a date.) The authors observed a solid response to the 2010 AAN guidelines, including "significant improvement" in adherence, most notably regarding

22. Hilary H. Wang et al., "Improving Uniformity in Brain Death Determination Policies over Time," *Neurology* 88.6 (February 7, 2017): 562–568, doi: 10.1212 /WNL.0000000000003597.

apnea and ancillary testing. Despite these gains, how-ever, variation persisted in other areas, in particular, specifying that the determination be made by a clinician trained in neurology or neurosurgery. While adherence has measurably improved over the past two decades, the authors conclude that more needs to be done. Despite the recent availability of promising tools and training modules, they suggest that regulatory oversight may be needed to attain uniformity, which cannot be guaran-teed through voluntary reporting alone.

Representative surveys as described above may most accurately depict nationwide performance, but the con-crete findings of a single institution are also valuable, particularly considering that a patient can be treated only at a single institution. Indeed, family members probably are more interested in how closely the institu-tion that is treating their loved one conforms to proper methodology. Therefore, it is worth relating the findings of a recent retrospective inquiry at an academic tertiary care center near Kansas City, Missouri.[23] The authors reviewed seventy-six cases of brain death in adults between 2011 and 2015 and found that, overall, strict adherence to the guidelines was correctly documented in 38 percent of the cases. Prerequisites to the clinical examination were accounted for in 54 percent, and an apnea test was completed in 39.5 percent. Of the twenty-three patients who did not receive an apnea test, fifteen did not undergo ancillary testing. Only 45 percent of

---

23. Ashutosh Pandey et al., "Variability in Diagnos-ing Brain Death at an Academic Medical Center," *Neuroscience Journal* 2017 (March 2, 2017), 1–7, doi: 10.1155/2017/6017958.

diagnoses were made by specialists in neurology or neu-rosurgery. Finally, the guidelines were strictly followed in only twenty-three of the thirty-nine cases involving organ donation. Based on these findings of considerable diagnostic variability, the hospital updated its policy with the aim of improving documentation.

The preponderance of available evidence leads to the clear conclusion that guideline variability and practice deviation constitute an enduring source of concern. Indeed, according to a 2016 review article by one of the authors of the 2010 AAN guidelines, the lack of uniformity creates "unacceptable variability and risks for falsely pronouncing a patient dead."[24] Other authors have asserted that "the personal experiences of provid-ers who perform such declarations" provide further, if anecdotal, evidence of practice variation.[25]

Inconsistent Clinical Practice

It is difficult to quantify the level of adherence to accepted standards, particularly since there is no uni-form operational protocol and representative evaluations of clinical practice have never been conducted. Writing in *Critical Care Medicine*, John Oropello of the Mount Sinai School of Medicine raised this very concern:

---

24. Panayiotis N. Varelas and Ariane Lewis, "Modern Approach to Brain Death," *Seminars in Neurology* 36.6 (December 2016): 625, doi: 10.1055/s-0036-1592317.

25. David Y. Hwang, Emily J. Gilmore, and David M. Greer, "Assessment of Brain Death in the Neurocritical Care Unit," *Neurosurgery Clinics of North America* 24.3 (July 2013): 473, doi: 10.1016/j.nec.2013.02.003.

"Although it is reasonable to assume that physicians conducting these examinations are sometimes making up for deficiencies in the policies, it is probable that deviations from protocol are an even greater source of variability and potential error."[26]

While it would not necessarily be surprising if, similar to other serious medical examinations, compliance with the accepted methods of determining death by the neurological criteria were to flag to a certain degree in ordinary practice, the gravity and finality of such a determination renders any lapses in vigilance repellent.[27] In 1984, one of the earliest studies on physicians' actual practice found widespread variability.[28] A "small but telling survey" from 2003 found that only "four of 10 centers and none of the eight surveyed neurosurgeons answered 'yes' to the question 'Do you follow guidelines/ waiting periods exactly?'"[29]

---

26. John M. Oropello, "Determination of Brain Death: Theme, Variations, and Preventable Errors," *Critical Care Medicine* 32.6 (June 2004): 1417, doi: 10.1097/01 .CCM.0000128962.56651.1C.

27. Powner, "Certification of Brain Death," 1587.

28. Peter McL. Black and Nicholas T. Zervas, "Declaration of Brain Death in Neurosurgical and Neurological Practice," *Neurosurgery* 15.2 (August 1984): 170, referenced in Choi et al., "Brain Death Revisited," 828.

29. James Fackler and Brahm Goldstein, "Pediatric Brain Death," *Critical Care Medicine* 39.9 (September 2011): 2197, doi: 10.1097/CCM.0b013e3182226fc7, referencing Matthew Y. Chang, Lori A. McBride, and Margaret A. Ferguson, "Variability in Brain Death Declaration Practices

A more recent study published in the December 2013 issue of *Neurology* reviewed the records of 226 adults from sixty-eight institutions in two states, whose organs were donated after a determination of brain death.[30] However, this assessment of clinical practice still is indirect, as it is a retrospective review of the medical records of deceased patients. Nevertheless, it yielded "a rough snapshot of the current state of the documentation of [brain death] determination in practice."

The AAN guidelines were strictly followed in 44.7 percent of cases and loosely followed in 37.2 percent. Adherence was deemed incomplete in 18.1 percent of cases. The absence of all brain-stem reflexes and motor responses to pain was completely documented in only 45.1 percent of cases. Apnea testing was completed in 73.5 percent of cases but for unknown reasons was not attempted in 20.8 percent. The authors speculate that the notable lack of apnea testing may be attributable to physicians' discomfort or unfamiliarity with current best practices.

Ancillary testing is recommended when apnea testing cannot be completed for any reason, yet 7 percent of patients whose apnea test was not completed were not given confirmatory ancillary tests. Four patients became

in Pediatric Head Trauma Patients," *Pediatric Neurosurgery* 39.1 (July 2003): 7–9, doi: 10.1159/000070871.

30. Claire N. Shappell et al., "Practice Variability in Brain Death Determination: A Call to Action," *Neurology* 31.23 (December 3, 2013): 2009–2014, doi: 10.1212/01.wnl.0000436938.70528.4a.

donors without undergoing either apnea or ancillary testing. In fact, the authors found that the decision to administer a particular test was often not based on a specific indication. On the contrary, several patients whose conditions indicated a particular test did not receive one. This led the researchers to conclude that the current use of ancillary testing "may be inefficient, or, at times, somewhat arbitrary." In 5.3 percent of cases, the specific mechanism leading to brain death was unclear or unknown—a finding the authors deemed "awkward," considering the AAN guidelines specify that brain death may be diagnosed only when the proximate cause is known and demonstrably irreversible. The authors noted that the AAN guidelines do not specify which confounding factors and their respective severities could preclude an examination or challenge a determination.

There is insufficient evidence to conclude that patients were incorrectly determined to be brain dead. Although many evaluations were incompletely documented, every chart did indicate catastrophic brain injury with characteristics consistent with brain death. The authors deem their findings to be a "conservative underestimate" because the cohort was limited to patients who became organ donors, and the analysis did not examine prerequisites or quality of adherence in any of the categories evaluated by the study. Their recommendations emphasize the need to clarify existing protocols, improve educational modules and methods of tracking performance and documentation, and develop practical tools such as a checklist. These important findings are generally consistent with the inferences that could be made from the several prior findings of variability in institutional guidelines.

Divergent Opinions on Death

There are ample indications that clinicians have divergent understandings regarding what constitutes brain death.[31] In fact, one survey indicates that 54 percent of medical directors and 44 percent of neurologists believe that patients in a persistent vegetative state should be considered dead.[32] Troubling as each instance of diagnostic error is, a far greater threat is presented by the ongoing proposals to broaden the definition of death to include the disabled and patients in a PVS—who are unquestionably alive—as candidates for organ harvesting.

Several other surveys have yielded similarly unsettling results concerning physicians' conception of brain death and their interpretation of the neurological criteria. For instance, a 2004–2006 survey of pediatric intensivists and pediatric and adult neurosurgeons in Canada found that more than half of the respondents expressed no concept of death that would justify the existing criteria for brain death. Of particular concern were the sizeable percentage of respondents (22 percent of pediatric intensivists and 20 percent of neurosurgeons) who used a future-oriented "prognosis" concept—the view that death or poor quality of life is inevitable— and the similarly sizeable percentage (17 percent of pediatric

---

31. Choi et al., "Brain Death Revisited," 824.

32. Wesley J. Smith, *Culture of Death* (New York: Encounter Books, 2000), 176.

intensivists and 27 percent of neurosurgeons) who used a higher-brain concept of death.[33]

These findings were echoed in a 2012 survey of American neurologists, which found that respondents did not share a consistent rationale for accepting brain death as death and expressed inconsistent interpretations of various diagnostic features. Almost half of the respondents articulated a higher-brain concept of death. Only 45 percent of the neurologists indicated that both brain death and cardiac death signify the death of the patient.[34]

At the least, such findings suggest a lack of adequate formation on the criteria and rationale for brain death. Although the opinions reflected in this survey are not necessarily predictive of error, they nonetheless may be loosely interpreted as proxy indicators of actual practice. This is obviously problematic because they diverge considerably from the guidelines. Therefore, if a practitioner makes a determination of death on the basis of higher-brain damage or the patient's poor prognosis at the time of the examination, rather than a thorough "by the book" evaluation of the patient's actual status, there is the threatening possibility that death could be declared prematurely.

---

33. Ari R. Joffe, "Is There Good Justification for the Universal Medical Acceptance of Brain Death as Death?," *APA Newsletter on Philosophy and Medicine* 9.1 (Fall 2009): 10.

34. Ari R. Joffe et al., "A Survey of American Neurologists about Brain Death: Understanding the Conceptual Basis and Diagnostic Tests for Brain Death," *Annals of Intensive Care* 2 (2012), 4, doi: 10.1186/2110-5820-2-4.

We have other indications that brain death determinations "often are performed incorrectly," which is not to say, however, that they are "inherently unreliable." In a meta-analysis conducted by Bernat and Wijdicks, more than half of ninety-three children who were classified as brain-dead were diagnosed using criteria that deviated from established guidelines. Thirty-eight patients became organ donors, but procurement was halted in twenty other cases following a neurological examination.[35]

Efforts to Improve Adherence

Indeed, efforts are underway to ameliorate this situation. These include addressing the clinical competence of physicians in conducting brain death examinations, an area that has not been well studied. Considering the complexity of the clinical examination, Benjamin MacDougall and colleagues conclude that the prevailing "laxity is alarming."[36] They devised a training course on how to properly determine death according to the AAN parameters, which they used to assess physicians' knowledge and identify practice gaps at Yale–New Haven Health System, their home institution. The training consisted of a forty-minute instructional session on all facets of the determination, including the identification

35. Eelco F. M. Wijdicks and James Bernat, "Chronic 'Brain Death': Meta-analysis and Conceptual Consequences," reply to Antonio López-Navidad, *Neurology* 53.6 (October 12, 1999): 1369, doi: 10.1212/WNL.53.6.1369.

36. Benjamin J. MacDougall et al., "Simulation-Based Training in Brain Death Determination," *Neurocritical Care* 21.3 (December 2014): 384, doi: 10.1007/s12028 -014-9975-x.

of confounders and signs that would preclude a determination of death. The instructional period was followed
by a simulation exercise.

Participants' knowledge was measured by a baseline
pretest and a post-training assessment. Physicians representing multiple specialties performed rather poorly on
the pretest, with an average score of 41.5 percent. This
was particularly disquieting, even if neurologists and
neurosurgeons scored significantly higher than other
specialists. The scores on the post-training assessment
were considerably higher.[37] The authors suggest that it
would be sensible for other institutions to adopt this type
of model as an effective and efficient means of improving
performance. Other simulation models designed specifically to improve the recognition of confounders have
also been developed and appear similarly promising.[38]

The clinical examination is reliable, but determining
brain death is a "complex process that requires experience and diligence."[39] Untrained clinicians are unlikely
to master the entire process, as the results of this training
attest. Indeed, important details of the process, such
as properly accounting for the confounding effect of
intoxication, may benefit from specialized expertise.

The American College of Medical Toxicology
recently weighed in on the tricky matter of assessing

37. Ibid., 389.

38. Sara Hocker et al., "Testing Confounders in Brain
Death Determination: A New Simulation Model," *Neurocritical Care* 23.3 (December 2015): 401–408, doi:
10.1007/s12028-015-0130-0.

39. Varelas and Lewis, "Approach to Brain Death," 625.

patients presenting with a drug overdose. Suggesting there may be some limitations to the AAN approach, the college recommended consulting with a medical or clinical toxicologist in cases where brain death is suspected but intoxication remains unclear. The college reasoned that screening tests are not comprehensive enough to detect all the drugs that cause a depressed mental status. Furthermore the use of five drug half-lives as the standard means of calculating clearance may not be stringent enough in every case. This is particularly true for patients who have received an exceedingly high dose of a toxicant, because even a small percentage of such an overdose could be potent enough to produce clinical effects. In some cases, coma resembling brain death has lasted up to seven days following baclofen overdose, which is much longer than would be expected using the typical calculation based on five half-lives.[40]

Other factors can complicate the picture as well, such as altered pharmacokinetics among patients with organ failure, co-exposure to other agents, and the presence of various conditions that slow drug absorption or metabolism. Given these types of potential complications and the requirement to establish a proximate and irreversible cause of brain injury, the college recommends that patients presenting with an overdose should not be examined for brain death.

This word of caution takes on added relevance considering the burgeoning opioid epidemic plaguing the

40. Mark J. Neavyn et al., "ACMT Position Statement: Determining Brain Death in Adults after Drug Overdose," *Journal of Medical Toxicology* 13.3 (September 2017): 272, doi: 10.1007/s13181-017-0606-8.

United States, which could increase the incidence of potential brain death cases. Yet fentanyl, which accounts for a considerable percentage of overdoses, is one of the synthetic opioids that a typical opiate screening test does not identify.[41]

International Variability

The kinds of discrepancies found in the United States are abundantly evident at the international level as well. Indeed, a major 2015 survey of ninety-one countries found "surprisingly high" divergence from the AAN criteria. Fifty-three percent of standards in surveyed nations contained a protocol out of line with at least one recommended component of the clinical examination.[42] Methods of apnea testing varied widely as well. It is worth noting that the presence of a transplantation network was more indicative of the existence of a brain-death protocol than was the country's per-capita income.

This should not be discounted lightly, since a recent study observed considerable variation in the timing of the determination of death both within and between European countries. In Poland, for example, "there is a striking variation in brain death diagnosis between regions with low and high donation rates."[43]

---

41. Ibid.

42. Sarah Wahlster et al., "Brain Death Declaration: Practices and Perceptions Worldwide," *Neurology* 84.18 (May 5, 2015): 1872, doi: 10.1212/WNL.0000000000001540.

43. Giuseppe Citerio and Paul G. Murphy, "Brain Death: The European Perspective," *Seminars in Neurology* 35.2 (April 2015): 141, doi: 10.1055/s-0035-1547533.

In countries where more than one clinical examination is required, the observational period between them ranged from one hour in Denmark to twelve hours in Greece and Lithuania. Nonetheless, European nations share a fundamental understanding of the neurological criteria: absence of brain stem reflexes, inability to breathe, and unconsciousness. Given the range of technical components involved in the determination of brain death and the cultural, religious, and legal differences between countries, however, it is doubtful that a global consensus can be reached on the neurological criteria.[44] Commenting on these findings, Bernat argues that discrepancies in the United States stem from ingrained practices and practitioner bias rather than from cultural, religious, or legal factors that may account for variation internationally.[45] He also suggests that one potential but less discussed source of variation may be the disagreement over the legitimacy of brain death.

There are other noteworthy indications of persisting variability. Although an evaluation of the quality of brain-death determination in four Canadian pediatric intensive care units (ICUs) between 1999 and 2003 indicated that most examinations followed contemporary recommendations, the authors identified areas of deviation: 19 percent of the patients had only one examination, 18 percent were not tested for apnea, and 36 percent received only one apnea test. Many of these patients were declared brain-dead without ancillary tests

---

44. Wahlster et al., "Brain Death Declaration," 1870–1879.

45. James Bernat, "Comment: Is International Consensus on Brain Death Achievable?," in ibid., 1878.

whether or not they became organ donors. The authors were concerned by this lack of adherence to the legal requirements for an apnea test and two clinical exams. Even though the need for a second examination has been debated, among patients who did have two exams, the waiting period between them was often shorter than the recommended interval.[46]

The study also measured the differences between the two examinations. These findings were "reassuring," as there were no discrepancies in 109 of the 110 (99.1%) cases.[47] Nonetheless, the single exception may indicate the need for two valid exams. Even if some potential donors are lost as a result of that requirement, accuracy and public trust take precedence.[48] The authors recommended not only establishing national guidelines but also providing checklists as a means of improving the thoroughness of the examination. Incidentally, the concern that some organ donors may be lost because of the extra time required to conduct a second exam points to the precarious condition of most brain-dead bodies even if prolonged somatic maintenance has occurred in some cases. These findings are relatively consistent with earlier ones. The authors cite another multicenter study,

---

46. Ari R. Joffe et al., "Brain Death in Canadian PICUs: Demographics, Timing, and Irreversibility," *Pediatric Critical Care Medicine* 14.1 (January 2013): 4, 7, 8. See also Paul Shore, "Following Guidelines for Brain Death Examinations: A Matter of Trust," *Pediatric Critical Care Medicine* 14.1 (January 2013): 98, doi: 10.1097/PCC.0b013e31826775bb.

47. Joffe et al., "Brain Death in Canadian PICUs," 7.

48. Shore, "Following Guidelines for Brain Death," 98.

in which 25 percent of the clinical exams did not include an apnea test, 22 percent documented incomplete apnea testing, and only 12 percent satisfied the local requirement of two exams and two apnea tests.[49]

Internationally, "major diversity in clinical criteria has evolved" as well.[50] In 2002, Wijdicks published the results of a survey of eighty countries, seventy of which had practice guidelines in place. The good news is that each of these guidelines specifically highlighted the essential elements of the determination: the absence of confounding factors, motor response, and brain-stem reflexes and the presence of irreversible coma. Wijdicks concluded that while there is global consensus on the legitimacy of brain death, there are differences in the means by which it is determined, including the specific procedures followed, the experience and specialization of physicians, the role of confirmatory tests, and the method of testing for apnea. The clear implication of these findings is that further standardization is desirable.

He found "major differences" in several categories, such as the number, experience, and specialties of physicians empowered to make the determination. For example, only half of the guidelines required more than one physician. There was great variation and, in some cases, a total lack of specification regarding the observation period after declaration of brain death. Furthermore,

---

49. Rodrigo E. Mejia and Murray M. Pollack, "Variability in Brain Death Determination Practices in Children," *JAMA* 274.7 (August 16, 1995): 551, 552, doi: 10.1001 /jama.1995.03530070048028, referenced in Joffe et al., "Brain Death in Canadian PICUs," 7.

50. Wijdicks, "Brain Death Worldwide," 23.

only 40 percent of the guidelines mandated confirmatory laboratory testing. This is particularly pronounced in Europe, where such tests are required in eleven of their twenty-five guidelines but are used at least in complementary fashion in all the others.[51] With the notable exception of Sweden, the actual selection of particular confirmatory tests "seems to be arbitrary."[52] However, all the European guidelines stress that brain death is principally a clinical determination.[53]

Of great concern was Wijdick's finding that apnea testing was noticeably inconsistent and was recommended in only 59 percent of the countries.[54] There are extreme examples in Central and South America where tests have no specified criteria or the examination relies solely on disconnecting the patient from the ventilator. On the premise that inducing "acute hypercarbia to maximally stimulate the respiratory centers" is the accepted standard for documenting apnea, he surmised that in half of the eighty countries surveyed, "the apnea

---

51. Ibid., 21.

52. Eelco F. M. Wijdicks, "The Clinical Criteria of Brain Death throughout the World: Why Has It Come to This?," *Canadian Journal of Anesthesia* 53.6 (June 2006): 541, doi: 10.1007/BF03021842. He specifies that "in Sweden, a cerebral angiogram has to be performed twice, with an adequate period of observation in between, documenting an absence of blood flow to the brain."

53. Nicolas G. Guignard et al., "Brain Death Determination in Australia and New Zealand: A Survey of Intensive Care Units," *Critical Care and Resuscitation* 13.4 (December 2011): 273.

54. Wijdicks, "Brain Death Worldwide," 21.

test is not performed adequately."[55] Considering the fundamental need to establish apnea, this type of variation must be corrected if an international standard is to be achieved.[56] Another notable inconsistency is that India and Hong Kong follow the United Kingdom's brain-stem-death standard. China, incidentally, has no legal criteria, and in other countries, "the guidelines seem unnecessarily complicated."[57] Commenting on this landmark survey, leading international practitioners described the differences as "stunning" and "troubling."

Despite updates to guidelines in both the United States and Canada, "considerable practice variation" remains.[58] A cross-sectional study of guidelines used in ICUs and organ procurement organizations in Canada revealed inconsistencies in key components of the determination. For instance, only 31 percent of adult guidelines and 18 percent of pediatric guidelines contained all potential confounding factors; only 65 percent of adult guidelines included tests for all brain stem reflexes; components of the apnea test were omitted, particularly the need to document hypercarbic stimulation of the respiratory center; and most protocols did not specify a waiting time before conducting the first examination.[59]

---

55. Ibid., 24.

56. M. Smith, "Brain Death," i8.

57. Wijdicks, "Brain Death Worldwide," 21, 24.

58. Jeanne Teitelbaum and Sam D. Shemie, "Neurologic Determination of Death," *Neurologic Clinics* 29.4 (November 2011): 787, doi: 10.1016/j.ncl.2011.08.003.

59. Karen Hornby et al., "Variability in Hospital-Based Brain Death Guidelines in Canada," *Canadian Journal*

Half of the guidelines that specified when death should be declared indicated that it should be after the first clinical examination. This is unsettling in part because it is not clear whether a second exam is still required when organ procurement is not a factor: "Considerable confusion would be generated if it were widely known that some institutions in Canada determine death after the first examination, while others wait until the second."[60]

This survey, like the others of its kind, only assessed guidance documents and therefore does not directly reflect actual practice. Nevertheless, the authors reasonably extrapolate that "it is possible that practitioners could compensate for this variability; however we speculate that actual practice has greater variation."[61] Given the consequences of a false determination, they conclude that the evident inconsistency at the institutional level reinforces the need for standardization. According to another Canadian survey, 96 percent of physicians felt that a revised national standard and an accompanying checklist would be useful.[62]

---

of Anesthesia 53.6 (June 2006): 615, 617, doi: 10.1007/BF03021854.

60. Ibid., 618.

61. Ibid.

62. Christopher James Doig et al., "Brief Survey: Determining Brain Death in Canadian Intensive Care Units," *Canadian Journal of Anesthesia* 53.6 (June 2006): 611, doi: 10.1007/BF03021853.

4

Case Reports

Since the human element is involved, the determination of brain death is open not only to error but also to abuse. Mistakes can happen with any diagnosis, but the stakes cannot get any higher than a diagnosis of death. The prospect for abuse is also a persistent threat, demanding equally constant vigilance. Error and abuse are thus obvious concerns, particularly since there is no uniform, universally followed set of standards. How accurately and consistently the determination of brain death is actually made is thus a matter of great weight even if it is not readily quantifiable.

From time to time, cases of error do surface in the press. However, these often have limited value because their lack of details makes it difficult to ascertain with precision where an error was made. Furthermore, these relatively isolated reports do not help us ascertain the overall level of conformity to accepted guidelines for determining death. Nevertheless, some of these accounts are instructive in many respects. At the least, they remind us that errors do occur. Several cases point to important elements of the determination process, such as the need to account for confounding factors and the need for the medical team and the media to use precise language.

Although mistakes happen, the determination of death by neurological criteria is widely viewed as a reliable diagnosis, and there have been no confirmed reports of a patient recovering when the neurological examination was conducted properly. Nevertheless, some important concerns about its application remain. Saying "brain death *is* death" is one thing. Equally true, however, is the troubling correlation that by declaring someone brain dead incorrectly, a living person is declared legally dead. A single case in which a person unequivocally meets the neurological criteria for death but subsequently recovers would invalidate the whole concept of brain death. Naturally, the prospect of any such occurrence has been monitored over the years.

Shortly after the Harvard Ad Hoc Committee adopted the neurological criteria in 1968, several studies were undertaken around the globe to assess and fine-tune the clinical tests used to make the determination that a patient has suffered complete and irreversible loss of brain function. These inquiries included the examination of published instances of recovery. Writing in *Angelicum* in 1990, Philip Smith noted that this yielded a strikingly uniform conclusion: "In every case where recovery was claimed, the patient failed to meet one or more of the criteria."[1]

---

1. Philip Smith, "Brain Death: A Thomistic Appraisal," *Angelicum* 67 (1990): 29.

While preparing to update its guidelines in 2010, the American Academy of Neurology looked at peer-reviewed journals and other published accounts for evidence of patients who recovered neurological function after meeting the clinical criteria for brain death. The AAN found that among adults, "recovery of neurologic function has not been reported after the clinical diagnosis of brain death has been established using the criteria given in the 1995 AAN practice parameter."[2] Therefore, the academy concluded that the neurological criteria have not been invalidated. A similar conclusion was reached by researchers in Australia and New Zealand, who found no evidence that brain death had been misdiagnosed when clinicians followed the guidelines of the Australian and New Zealand Intensive Care Society.[3]

Collectively, these studies have examined more than forty years' worth of determinations. Ten thousand cases have been confirmed in the United Kingdom alone over the past decade. In every instance of prolonged somatic maintenance—particularly in Japan, where it occurs more frequently and where people have been reluctant to accept brain death—no evidence of recovery is apparent. This historical record indicates that the diagnostic

---

2. Eelco F. M. Wijdicks et al., "Evidence-Based Guideline Update: Determining Brain Death in Adults—Report of the Quality Standards Subcommittee of the American Academy of Neurology," *Neurology* 74.23 (June 8, 2010): 1912, doi: 10.1212/WNL.0b013e3181e242a8.

3. Nicolas G. Guignard et al., "Brain Death Determination in Australia and New Zealand: A Survey of Intensive Care Units," *Critical Care and Resuscitation Journal* 13.4 (December 2011): 271–273.

standard is reliable.[4] Nevertheless, carelessness and error can easily create the impression that the entire concept of brain death is baseless and corrupt, particularly in the context of organ transplantation, where allegations of abuse are especially disturbing.

Aggressive Organ Procurement

In 2012, a lawsuit filed in Manhattan's Supreme Court claimed that the New York Organ Donor Network "procured organs without performing legally required tests and from individuals who still showed signs of life."[5] The allegations were made by Patrick McMahon, a former transplant coordinator for the organization, who claimed he was fired for protesting the prevailing *modus operandi*. What precisely is meant by *signs of life* is not specified. But that is what makes all the difference.

It is not clear from the few publically available details whether the claims have a basis in fact. The general nature of the allegation and the brief descriptions of these cases provided in the press make it impossible for any outsider to reach a firm conclusion. These are, however, disturbing allegations worth taking seriously. The legal case has not been resolved, in large part because it hinges on the status of four patients' medical records. By law, medical records are considered private when held

---

4. D. Gardiner et al., "An International Perspective on the Diagnosis of Death," *British Journal of Anaesthesia* 108 suppl 1 (January 2012): i14–i28, doi: 10.1093/bja/aer397.

5. *McMahon v. New York Organ Donor Network*, __ A.D.3d __, 2018 NY Slip Op 03820 (N.Y. A.D. 1st Dept, May 29, 2018).

by hospitals, but their status is more ambiguous when they are in the possession of an organ procurement organization. In 2017, the court ruled that, like in hospitals, medical records at OPOs are confidential. But New York law also allows confidential records to be disclosed in whistleblower cases. Given that exception, the judge sided with McMahon and ordered the New York Organ Donor Network to turn over redacted records that omit identifying patient information. The organization has appealed this ruling.[6]

In 2007, the *Los Angeles Times* published a special report about another erroneous determination of death. A forty-seven-year-old Fresno man suffered catastrophic brain hemorrhage (an inoperable Pontine bleed) and had "almost no hope of recovery."[7] He was pronounced brain-dead by two physicians as specified by California law. The second physician seemed in a rush according to the patient's daughter, and she grew suspicious. A nurse then conducted her own examination and found clinical symptoms inconsistent with brain death, such as strong gag and cough reflexes and slight head movement.

A third physician, a neurologist, determined that the patient was not brain-dead. He did not directly address the prior exams, but he said, "I know what I did was

6. Judy C. Semeci, "New York's Appellate Division Rules on Confidentiality of Organ Procurement Organization Records," *National Law Review*, June 7, 2018, https://www.natlawreview.com/; and *McMahon v. New York Organ Donor Network*.

7. Charles Ornstein and Tracy Weber, "Close Call in Death Ruling of Potential Organ Donor," *Los Angeles Times*, April 12, 2007, http://articles.latimes.com/.

right." The patient was, in fact, still alive at the time of these examinations, although he died eleven days later. Since the patient's family had agreed to donate his organs, the error raised concerns that "doctors might be compromising the care of prospective donors."[8] The *LA Times* clearly relates that the daughter felt pressured to proceed with organ donation, although other family members did not feel coerced.

It is routine for hospital personnel to alert the regional organ donor network of a potential candidate. In response to this case, the executive director of California's Organ Transplant Network indicated that her staff had concerns about the legitimacy of the determination, and therefore organ extraction would not have proceeded. However, the *LA Times* reported that the donor network's confidential case notes did not include these concerns. Regarding the notes in the patient's hospital records, Michael Williams, the chairman of the AAN ethics committee, stated, "If the documentation is correct, they should never ever have considered the possibility of brain death for that patient. ... It's not even close."[9]

To cite another case, a family filed a lawsuit over the determination of death of their eighteen-year-old son. A snowboarding accident led to his hospitalization, and five days later, the family was told he was brain dead. With that understanding, they consented to organ donation, which proceeded as planned. According to *ABC News*, brain death allegedly was not recorded at

---

8. Ibid.
9. Ibid.

the time of examination. Rather, it was documented retrospectively the following day when life support was being withdrawn in anticipation of organ harvesting. For this reason, the family claims that their son was not actually declared dead prior to the preparation for organ procurement. The hospital did acknowledge that a mistake was made in recording the time of death but called it "an error in documentation."[10] Otherwise, it insists that everything was done by the book. The error in documentation in this case could be interpreted as either highly suspicious or as a simple oversight. Nevertheless, it is not difficult to appreciate that any genuine instance of error, carelessness, or abuse might never be detected in the context of organ donation.

Thorough documentation of brain death is an area of significant concern. One review of the records from Los Angeles County General Hospital found inconsistencies in the notation of the exam. For example, corneal reflex and motor responses was documented in only 57 percent and 66 percent of the cases, respectively.[11] As others have noted, we simply do not know whether these findings reflect careless documentation or unreliable clinical examinations. Regardless, they provide

10. Susan Donaldson James, "Patients' Hospital Lawsuit Says Teen Was 'Killed' for Organs," *ABC News*, March 6, 2009, http://abcnews.go.com/.

11. Michael Y. Wang et al., "Brain Death Documentation: Analysis and Issues," *Neurosurgery* 51.3 (September 2002): 734, doi: 10.1227/01.NEU.0000024156.53597.1A.

compelling evidence that quality-assurance activities must be improved.[12]

Declaring Brain Death on
the Basis of Poor Prognosis

Other cases involve startling recoveries from severe neurological injuries with a poor prognosis. A common feature of many of these stories is suspicion on the part of family members that, at the very least, corners had been cut for the sake of pursuing the overriding objective of organ donation.

For example, a nineteen-year-old Danish girl was hospitalized after a car accident and "slipped into a coma." Doctors advised that "brain death would probably occur within days."[13] On that basis, they suggested withdrawing life support and proceeding with organ donation. Her parents consented, but when they took her off the ventilator, she continued to breathe on her own. Her recovery progressed from there. The hospital later acknowledged the "grave error in diagnosis" and conceded that the subject of organ donation should not have been broached, since "there were no clear signs that brain death would occur."[14]

---

12. Ibid., 735–736; and Eelco F. M. Wijdicks, "The Clinical Criteria of Brain Death throughout the World: Why Has It Come to This?," *Canadian Journal of Anesthesia* 53.6 (June 2006): 540–543, doi: 10.1007/BF03021842.

13. Thaddeus Baklinski, "Film on Teen Who Awoke from Coma before Having Organs Harvested Stirs 'Brain Death' Debate," *LifeSite News*, October 18, 2012, https://www.lifesitenews.com/.

14. Ibid.

Another case illustrates both the aggressive manner in which some physicians pursue organ donation as well as the importance of accounting for confounding factors. Two days after being injured in a car crash that killed his friend, seventeen-year-old Steven Thorpe was declared brain dead by a team of specialists. Thorpe was in an induced coma, and the physicians told his parents, "You need to start thinking about organ donations."[15] His parents refused and demanded another opinion. A neurologist was brought in to conduct an independent investigation, and he concluded that Thorpe was not brain dead. He was released from the hospital five weeks later after making an almost complete recovery.

This story is loaded with implications. Did the barbiturates used to induce coma interfere with Thorpe's neuronal function and therefore the determination of death? One of the core prerequisites for conducting the clinical examination is that the coma be irreversible and its cause known.[16] Did physicians not account for that, conduct an apnea test, or pursue any other measures do determine whether Thorpe could survive?

The hospital spokesman's imprecise characterization of the incident—note the word *almost*—may also be telling: "The injury to Steven's brain was extremely critical and several CT scans of the head showed almost irreversible damage."[17] When interviewed about the case, Julia

---

15. Hannah Furness, "'Miracle Recovery' of Teen Declared Brain Dead by Four Doctors," *Telegraph*, April 25, 2012, https://www.telegraph.co.uk/.

16. Wijdicks et al., "Determining Brain Death," 1914.

17. Furness, "Miracle Recovery."

Piper, a general practitioner who was instrumental in securing the second examination, said, "I am astonished with the outcome, but one worries that this may happen more often than we know."[18]

Diagnostic Errors

In addition to claims of systematic abuse, there are reliable accounts of serious errors in making the determination of death. In July 2013, a particularly egregious case from 2009 came to light. A woman at St. Joseph's hospital, in Syracuse, New York, was pronounced brain dead, but she woke up just before her organs were to be harvested.[19]

In this case, there clearly appear to have been multiple lapses throughout the determination process. The patient arrived at the hospital following a drug overdose, which is one of the confounding factors that must be excluded or properly accounted for prior to making a determination of death, because intoxicants can suppress brain function and thereby mimic brain death. Such a state is reversible, whereas the authentic death of the entire brain is not.

18. Louise Eccles, "The Boy Who Came Back from the Dead: Experts Said Car Crash Teen Was beyond Hope. His Parents Disagreed," *Daily Mail*, April 24, 2012, https://www.dailymail.co.uk/health/article-2134346/Steven-Thorpe-Teenager-declared-brain-dead-FOUR-doctors-makes-miracle-recovery.html?printingPage=true.

19. John O'Brien and James T. Mulder, "St. Joe's 'Dead' Patient Awoke as Docs Prepared to Remove Organs," *Post-Standard*, updated July 9, 2013, http://www.syracuse.com/.

An official report issued by the US Centers for Medicare and Medicaid Services clearly specifies the hospital's manifold failures in this case. First of all, the patient "did not meet criteria for withdrawal of care." Not only was she not brain-dead, but she had not suffered a cardiopulmonary arrest. Furthermore, "insufficient time had elapsed and insufficient testing was done to make sure all drugs were out of the patient's system before withdrawal of life-sustaining treatment was discussed."[20] Not only did physicians fail to take these steps, but they also elected to forego recommended treatment to counteract the absorption of the drugs the patient had taken.

Other red flags went unheeded. A nurse observed that the patient exhibited reflexes inconsistent with brain death and even appeared to breathe independently: "Toes curled when foot stimulated, tachycardic, hypertensive, flaring nostrils, mouthing with lips and moving tongue, breathing above the ventilator." But this did not trigger any sort of reevaluation. If this were not chilling enough, the patient, despite these observations, was soon thereafter injected with a sedative.[21] It is hard to account for such a move.

The hospital did not react well after the fact either. Despite the gravity of the case, it undertook no internal investigation to understand what went wrong and to

20. US Centers for Medicare and Medicaid Services, "Statement of Deficiencies and Plan of Correction, St. Joseph's Hospital Health Center," OMB No. 0938-0391, June 11, 2011, 10, available at https://www.scribd.com/doc/148583905/U-S-Centers-for-Medicare-and-Medicaid-Services-report-on-St-Joe-s.

21. Ibid., 2–3.

prevent similar occurrences in the future. It managed only to produce a superficial one-page document that lacked suitable analysis and came only in response to an unannounced investigative visit from the state.

The entire organ transplantation enterprise is built on the trust that corners will not be cut. Trust is precisely what is eroded when cases like this occur. Great damage is done even if such horrific episodes are, as leading neurologist Eelco Wijdicks put it, "exceedingly rare."[22] He also indicated that this should not happen if all the proper steps are taken, which implies that clear and standardized protocols should be routinely followed. Aside from the fact that individual institutions follow different protocols for determining brain death, there is no system for reporting medical errors, except by coming forward as a whistleblower like McMahon, and consequently no way to know the true incidence of such near catastrophes.

The following dramatic case also rattled nerves. In 2008, a young Oklahoma man was in a serious off-road accident and airlifted to a hospital in Texas. His case generated considerable attention because he was declared brain-dead but later recovered. He even recalls medical personnel discussing his death and the prospect of organ transplantation, to which his grieving family had consented. The first sign that he was not actually dead came when a relative elicited a strong reaction from him

---

22. Sydney Lupkin, "Patient Wakes Up as Doctors Get Ready to Remove Organs," *ABC News*, July 9, 2013, https://abcnews.go.com/.

by scraping his foot with the edge of a pocketknife.[23] It is unclear why such signs of life were not detected in the official clinical examination, which the hospital maintained it performed correctly.

Another important aspect of this case has some bearing on the role of ancillary tests. A television documentary indicated that at an unspecified point in their evaluation, doctors confirmed their assessment of brain death using an ancillary test. According to those results, the patient apparently exhibited no cerebral blood flow.[24] In this case, therefore, the reliance on that blood flow test at that stage in the evaluation, combined with the lack of a proper and thorough clinical examination, may well have yielded an erroneous determination of death.[25]

Confounding Factors

Many cases in which brain death has been misdiagnosed involve the presence of a condition such as hypothermia, intoxication, or metabolic disturbance, which is known to be a confounding factor and should preclude any determination of death unless properly accounted for.

23. Dan Coffin, interviewed by Natalie Morales, "'Dead' Man Recovering after ATV Accident," transcript, *Dateline*, March 23, 2008, http://www.nbcnews.com/.

24. Pam Dunlap and Doug Dunlap, interviewed by Natalie Morales, "'Dead' Man Recovering after ATV Accident."

25. The clinical examination should detect brain-mediated reflexes. With respect to the role of blood tests, Sweden requires two cerebral angiograms with an observation period in between.

In 2011, *Critical Care Medicine* published a case study that alleged to be the first documented "reversal of a diagnosis of brain death made in full adherence to American Academy of Neurology guidelines."[26] The patient in this case, a fifty-five-year-old man, suffered a heart attack. Following cardiopulmonary resuscitation, spontaneous circulation was restored, and a routine but relatively new therapy called therapeutic hypothermia was used to maximize the likelihood of an improved neurologic outcome. This is essentially the only intervention demonstrated to be effective in patients who remain comatose despite the return of spontaneous circulation following cardiac arrest.[27] Once the patient was rewarmed to 36.5°C, however, neurological function was seriously compromised, and it deteriorated further over the next twenty-four hours. At this point, the neurological examination indicated brain death.

A subsequent examination and an apnea test both confirmed the diagnosis. However, hypothermia, like drug intoxication, is a well-established confounding factor that needs to be excluded before a declaration of brain death can be made. The family agreed to organ donation. When the patient was taken to the operating room twenty-four hours after death had been declared,

26. Adam C. Webb and Owen B. Samuel, "Reversible Brain Death after Cardiopulmonary Arrest and Induced Hypothermia," *Critical Care Medicine* 39.6 (June 2011): 1538, doi: 10.1097/CCM.0b013e3182186687.

27. David M. Greer and Gioacchino G. Curiale, "End-of-Life and Brain Death in Acute Coma and Disorders of Consciousness," *Seminars in Neurology* 33.2 (April 2013): 158, doi: 10.1055/s-0033-1348959.

he had regained corneal and cough reflexes and spontaneous respirations. The authors emphatically concluded that clinicians should use "caution in the determination of brain death after cardiac arrest when induced hypothermia is used," including the use of confirmatory testing and a minimum observation period.[28]

This case naturally created a lot of waves, but it was not the exception its authors advertised it to be, and for that reason, they came under sharp criticism. In a letter to the editor titled "There Is No Reversible Brain Death," a team of prominent neurologists challenged not only how the case was presented in the literature, but how the neurological examination was conducted. Citing the longstanding, well-understood preconditions for proceeding to a clinical neurologic exam, the critics noted that it is "very concerning" that the authors did not, in fact, follow the AAN guidelines, which clearly stipulate that confounders be excluded and "even specifically [mention] the dangers of assessing patients with hypothermia after cardiopulmonary resuscitation." To claim, therefore, as the authors did, that the neurological examination conformed to the AAN guidelines is "very misleading." Given the significance of therapeutic hypothermia, the critics went one step further than the study authors, maintaining that, "in fact, no neurologist should even try" to proceed with a neurological examination under those circumstances.[29] In light of these crucial factors and the confusion and doubt generated by this

---

28. Webb and Samuels, "Reversible Brain Death," 1538.

29. Eelco F. M. Wijdicks et al., "There Is No Reversible Brain Death," *Critical Care Medicine* 39.9 (September 2011): 2205, doi: 10.1097/CCM.0b013e318222724e.

case study, another team of corresponding physicians suggested that "the most appropriate title would have been: 'Misdiagnosis of brain death after cardiopulmonary arrest and induced hypothermia.'"[30]

Because of a confounding factor that was not accounted for, this purportedly iconoclastic case does not shatter the concept of brain death as would an identical case in which hypothermia was not a factor. This case also may prompt one to wonder how well versed practitioners are in the confounding effects of therapeutic hypothermia. Finally, it drives home the absolute need to meticulously follow published guidance when examining a patient for brain death.[31]

James Bernat and Richard Freeman suggest a seventy-two-hour waiting period following rewarming, because metabolic encephalopathy caused by hypothermia can take days to be reversed. The procedure can slow the clearance of confounding drugs already in the patient's system. This suggestion has been corroborated by other experts, including the Swedish Resuscitation Council.[32]

30. Jeffrey Frank, Fernando Goldenberg, and Agnieszka Ardelt, "Brain Death: The Contemporary Neurological Imperative," *Critical Care Medicine* 39.11 (November 2011): 2589, doi: 10.1097/CCM.0b013e31822a5dcb.

31. M. Smith, "Brain Death: Time for an International Consensus," *British Journal of Anaesthesia* 108 suppl 1 (January 2012): i7–i8, doi 10.1093/bja/aer355.

32. Richard B. Freeman and James L. Bernat, "Ethical Issues in Organ Transplantation," *Progress in Cardiovascular Diseases* 55.3 (November–December 2012): 285, doi: 10.1016/j.pcad.2012.08.005. See also Tobias Cronberg et al., "Neurological Prognostication after Cardiac Arrest:

Others suggest an even longer waiting period of four to five days after cardiac arrest (although still seventy-two hours after rewarming).[33] This proposal is based in part on the remarkable late recovery of a man treated with induced hypothermia. On day three in the intensive care unit following rewarming, this man displayed many clinical signs consistent with brain death. On day four, his condition was still "abysmal," but he began to show steady improvement on days five and six. Eventually, he was discharged from the hospital with no neurological impairment. Had a formal brain death protocol been followed on day three, he probably would have been declared dead. This was not pursued, because of the confounding nature of therapeutic hypothermia.

Even in the absence of therapeutic hypothermia, certain precautions need to be taken when cardiac arrest, rather than primary trauma, leads to severe neurological impairment. The clinician must account for the underlying event responsible for a suspected case of brain death. "Neurologic assessment may be unreliable" in the acute phase after resuscitation following cardiorespiratory arrest because pupillary and motor responses can return in the first twenty-four hours.[34]

Recommendations from the Swedish Resuscitation Council," *Resuscitation* 84.7 (July 2013): 867–872, doi: 10.1016/j.resuscitation.2013.01.019.

33. Richard B. Arbour, "Brain Death: Assessment, Controversy, and Confounding Factors," *Critical Care Nurse* 33.6 (December 2013): 39, doi: 10.4037/ccn2013215.

34. Jeanne Teitelbaum and Sam Shemie, "Neurologic Determination of Death," *Neurologic Clinics* 29.4 (November 2011): 789, doi: 10.1016/j.ncl.2011.08.003.

Challenging a Determination of Brain Death

What if a determination of brain death is confirmed but the family refuses to accept its legitimacy? That is precisely what happened in the tragic case of Jahi McMath, a thirteen-year-old girl from Oakland, California. In December 2013, her tonsils were removed to alleviate her sleep apnea. Shortly afterward, she experienced profuse bleeding followed by cardiac arrest and brain damage. This catastrophic outcome is highly uncommon following such a procedure. Doctors determined a couple of days later that she was brain dead.

Her grieving family, however, was not convinced. By all accounts, poor communication on the part of the hospital did not help and may have played a role in escalating the conflict. Additional neurological examinations were conducted; these confirmed brain death. Her mother insisted that she could accept death if her daughter's heart stopped beating, but she could not do so on the basis of the neurological criteria. She invoked religious belief in support of this view and maintained the convicted hope that her daughter would recover.

The family took legal action to prevent the hospital from removing the ventilator. Since Jahi had been declared dead, the facility was under no legal obligation to keep her maintained by it. The court issued a stay and appointed the chief of pediatric neurology at Stanford University to conduct another independent examination. His examination also confirmed the determination of brain death. This constituted the sixth finding that she met the neurological criteria for death. The first two exams were conducted separately by hospital physicians, and an additional three were conducted by independent physicians at the family's request.[35]

Nevertheless, the judge issued a restraining order requiring the hospital to keep Jahi on the ventilator while the family sought another facility to maintain her body.[36] Such a transfer would require a tracheostomy and the insertion of gastrostomy tubes,[37] and most doctors and facilities want no part in operating on someone who is dead. Incidentally, previous legal decisions have over-ruled parents' refusal to discontinue ventilator support in the context of clearly established brain death.[38]

One facility in New Jersey, however, was willing to accommodate the McMaths, and a judge in California allowed Jahi's body to be transported across the country even though she was legally and medically dead. Following this transfer, the family's attorney intimated that he may pursue changes to California law, which links brain

35. Kristin J. Bender and Natalie Neysa Alund, "Judge Grants Restraining Order Keeping Brain Dead Oakland Girl on Ventilator through Monday," *Oakland Tribune*, updated August 12, 2016, https://www.mercurynews.com/.

36. Lisa Fernandez, "Deadline Looms to Take Jahi McMath off Ventilator," *NBC Bay Area*, December 30, 2013, https://www.nbcbayarea.com/.

37. Dana Ford, "Jahi McMath's Family Seeks to Move Brain-Dead Girl to Another Facility," *CNN.com*, updated December 27, 2013, https://www.cnn.com/.

38. Eun-Kyoung Choi et al., "Brain Death Revisited: The Case for a National Standard," *Journal of Law, Medicine and Ethics* 36.4 (Winter 2008): 828, doi: 10.1111/j.1748-720X.2008.00340.x.

death with ontological death. The argument is that the family, rather than hospital or judges, should make the determination.[39]

Alone among the fifty states, only New Jersey permits exceptions for those who object to brain death on religious grounds. Three other states—California, New York, and Illinois—allow for "reasonable accommodation" of religious objections or for conforming the time of death to the family's preference.[40] In Japan, known for its resistance to brain death, the neurological criteria became legalized in 1997, but only for those who wished to donate organs and whose families did not object.[41] In all other contexts, the long-standing Japanese preference for the cardiopulmonary criteria applies.

Particularly in the wake of tragedy and grief, flexibility and leniency toward family members are important components of a compassionate response. Nevertheless, allowing a religious exemption to the determination of death, as in New Jersey, "remains contentious."[42] Obvious

---

39. Matthias Gafni, "Jahi McMath: Could Her Case Change How California Determines Death?," *Bay Area News Group*, updated August 12, 2016, https://www.mercurynews.com/.

40. Ariane Lewis, Panayiotis Varelas, and David Greer, "Prolonging Support after Brain Death: When Families Ask for More," *Neurocritical Care* 24.3 (June 2016): 482, doi: 10.1007/s12028-015-0209-7.

41. Yutaka Kato, "Conscience in Health Care and the Definitions of Death," *Croatian Medical Journal* 54.1 (February 2013): 75, doi: 10.3325/cmj.2013.54.75.

42. Eelco F. M. Wijdicks, "Brain Death Worldwide: Accepted Fact But No Global Consensus in Diagnostic

ethical concerns and practical problems would arise if everyone could insist on their own criteria for death. One major ethical implication in clear-cut cases of brain death is the mistreatment of a corpse through chronic somatic maintenance, which is an "example of what science and technology could do, but should not do."[43] In fact, this is the principal ethical consideration; it applies to all patients, not just those considering organ donation.

In addition, if subjective views constitute sufficient grounds for granting a legitimate exception to the reality of death, they could also be invoked to reject the reality of life at its inception as scientifically corroborated by modern embryology. Similarly, patients could be declared dead while still alive. Some prominent bioethicists have recently argued that, given the persistent nature of the controversy over what constitutes death, people should be allowed to choose an available interpretation or standard that best corresponds to their beliefs, disposition, and values. This would include the higher-brain standard, which has yet to be legitimized anywhere.[44]

Criteria," *Neurology* 58.1 (January 2002): 24, doi: 10.1212 /WNL.58.1.20.

43. Claudio Crisci, comment on D. Alan Shewmon, "Chronic 'Brain Death': Meta-analysis and Conceptual Consequences," *Neurology* 53.6 (October 1999): 1370, doi: 10.1212/WNL.53.6.1369. See also Christopher J. G. Lang, comment on Shewmon, "Chronic 'Brain Death,'" *Neurology* 53.6 (October 1999): 1370–1371, doi: 10.1212 /WNL.53.6.1369.

44. Robert M. Veatch and Lainie F. Ross, *Defining Death: The Case for Choice* (Washington, DC: Georgetown University Press, 2016), 155.

The national discussion surrounding the case of Jahi McMath subsided for a while before new wrinkles reignited it. After being transferred out of state, her body continued to function in relative stability, which led some observers who had accepted the determination of death to form doubts about her status.[45] Her family claimed she could display limited responsiveness, and her family attorney petitioned the local California court, approximately ten months after she was first declared brain dead, for her to be declared alive again.

A decision by a judge to rescind the death certificate and declare that she is legally alive could have enormous implications. It could be taken to mean that the physicians who performed the clinical exam got it wrong back in 2013. If that were the case, it seems like it would be difficult to explain why all the subsequent examinations, particularly the last, court-mandated one—conducted under heightened media scrutiny—reached the same conclusion. Or it could be taken to mean that Jahi at some point no longer met the clinical criteria for brain death, which would be an unprecedented and inexplicable finding. Either way, such a legal declaration could seriously jeopardize the very determination of brain death altogether by calling into question the ability to determine it by the current clinical criteria. It raises the prospect that any family could simply reject the determination of death.

In fact, another family did directly question whether the clinical criteria are a satisfactory means of determining death. This case, from Nevada in 2015, was ultimately

---

45. Wesley J. Smith, "Justice for Jahi," *First Things*, September 15, 2017, https://www.firstthings.com/.

dropped because the patient, who was determined to be brain-dead but was nevertheless maintained on a ventilator as a result of legal intervention, subsequently underwent cardiac arrest and no longer could be maintained.[46]

In June 2018, something similar transpired with the McMath case. Jahi began to experience internal bleeding and liver failure. The family decided to remove her from the ventilator, resulting in a New Jersey declaration of death. This outcome may have provided a measure of closure, yet consequential legal ramifications regarding the petition to declare her alive may still be in play. The family is expected to continue pursuing a malpractice suit against the Oakland hospital, and responsibility for medical expenses incurred after she was declared brain-dead could be part of the verdict or settlement.[47] The outcome probably will hinge on whether Jahi should be considered legally alive or dead between the 2013 certification of death in California and the 2018 certification in New Jersey. A judge or jury may still be called on *ex post facto* to decide whether she continued to meet the neurological criteria.

The ripple effects of the McMath case are evident in other cases as well. For example, the attorney

---

46. Veatch and Ross, *Defining Death*, 57–59.

47. Samantha Schmidt, "Jahi McMath, the Calif. Girl in Life-Support Controversy, Is Now Dead," *Washington Post*, June 29, 2018, https://www.washingtonpost.com; and Matthias Gafni, "Jahi McMath Death Could Have Costly Implications in Civil Case against Hospital, Doctors," *Mercury News*, June 30, 2018, https://www.mercurynews .com.

representing Jahi's family was contacted by the father of a thirty-year-old woman who was declared brain dead at John Muir Medical Center near Oakland. He wanted to pursue his options to challenge that determination. The legal team was able to obtain a temporary restraining order in May 2015, preventing the hospital from withdrawing life support. The local court also ordered two independent examinations, which were conducted by neurologists from the University of California, San Francisco, School of Medicine. In an independent examination, two neurologists determined that she did not meet the clinical criteria for brain death.[48] This stands in contrast with the McMath case because the original determination was erroneous, although the reasons for this are not known publicly. Clearly, however, this alarming case has the potential to heighten a sense of uncertainty among the general public, encourage protests against declarations of brain death, and further unsettle matters on the legal front.

Given the repercussions of the McMath case, "New Jersey is considering elimination of their religious exception clause for determination of death by neurologic criteria."[49] A negotiated standard of death is undesirable, and it is not difficult to envision the chaos that could ensue. On the other hand, however, there are calls for

---

48. Matthias Gafni and David Debolt, "Walnut Creek Hospital Mistakenly Diagnoses Woman Brain-Dead," *East Bay Times*, updated August 16, 2016, https://www.eastbaytimes.com/.

49. Lewis et al., "Prolonging Support," 484.

the universal adoption of the New Jersey model.[50] For the time being, the status quo remains in place. A 2018 study found that religious exemptions occur very infrequently in New Jersey, with approximately thirty cases reported from 2012 to 2016.[51]

Although this scenario is uncommon, it is not unimportant. In thirteen cases at the Cleveland Clinic between 2005 and 2013, family members requested continued physiological support (a deviation from standard protocol) for patients who met the clinical criteria for brain death. This institution sought to make reasonable accommodations to the families even though it is in a state that does not legally require this. One problem, however, is that the rather vague standard of reasonable accommodation provides little concrete guidance and could result in arbitrary decision making as well as considerable distress for the clinical team. The Cleveland Clinic has proposed guidelines of its own to deal with such scenarios and has urged other institutions to proactively develop policies as well.[52]

50. L. Syd M. Johnson, "The Case for Reasonable Accommodation of Conscientious Objections to Declarations of Brain Death," *Journal of Bioethical Inquiry* 13.1 (March 2016): 105–115, doi: 10.1007/s11673-015-9683-z.

51. Rachel Grace Son and Susan M. Setta, "Frequency of Use of the Religious Exemption in New Jersey Cases of Determination of Brain Death," *BMC Medical Ethics* 19 (August 14, 2018): 76, doi: 10.1186/s12910-018-0315-0.

52. Anne Lederman Flamm, Martin L. Smith, and Patricia A. Mayer, "Family Members' Requests to Extend Physiologic Support after Declaration of Brain Death: A Case Series

Indeed, the whole matter of how institutions approach family objections to declarations of brain death was largely unexplored until a survey of 331 institutions representing half of the United States (including the four states that have laws or guidance concerning family objections) was conducted in 2015. Eighty percent of the protocols did not mention how to address family objections, but this proportion increased to 97 percent in the states without any existing laws.[53] The investigators of this survey likewise concurred that developing guidelines may be helpful.

Misleading Medical Reports

The bewilderment caused by error, abuse, and objections is reflected in and increased by many media stories involving brain death. The following case illustrates this widespread confusion. Relatives of a sixty-five-year-old woman were told she was brain dead after suffering a massive cerebral hemorrhage. An *Associated Press* story indicates that they took her home to make her comfortable before she died.[54] Other reports follow suit: "Her family had taken her home to die and were in the process

---

Analysis and Proposed Guidelines for Clinical Management," *Journal of Clinical Ethics* 25.3 (Fall 2014): 227–237.

53. Lewis et al., "Prolonging Support," 481, 482.

54. "Lake Elmo Woman, 65, Believed to Be Brain-Dead Recovers," *Associated Press*, updated November 14, 2015, available at https://www.twincities.com/.

of grieving and planning her funeral when she awoke and was rushed back to hospital."[55]

The first, most elementary thing to note is that corpses do not go home to die. This suggests that a formal declaration of death was not made. It seems a decision was made to remove life support, but that is not the same as a rigorous determination of death. Deciding that treatment is probably futile (a common occurrence) is a far cry from determining that the neurological criteria for death are satisfied (an uncommon occurrence). This case is also noteworthy because the patient was not an organ donor. The diagnostic error was made independently as it were. It seems likely that carelessness, at least, may have contributed to the error, but it cannot be attributed to the ulterior motive of organ harvesting.

There is one other telling aspect about this case. An *ABC News* story quotes Brad Helms, a physician at United Hospital, in St. Paul, Minnesota: "She had a huge bleed and was considered essentially brain-dead."[56] Perhaps this type of remark, communicated directly to the family, was the source of confusion. Even in the absence of additional facts about her precise condition, that type of statement itself is of great concern because there is no such thing as "essentially brain-dead." Successful communication is part of the physician's craft.

---

55. Hilary White, "Woman Diagnosed as 'Brain Dead' Walks and Talks after Awakening," *LifeSite News*, February 15, 2008, http://www.lifesitenews.com.

56. "Medical Miracle: Woman Back from Brink of Death," *ABC News*, February 14, 2008, https://www.abcnews .go.com.

In cases such as this, delicacy as well as precision must be maintained.

In 2008 a fifty-nine-year-old West Virginia woman woke up after doctors allegedly had declared her dead. No details were provided about the thoroughness of the clinical examination, so any reaction to the news report was bound to be speculative. But one assertion seems particularly difficult to credit: "Rigor mortis had set in while Mrs. Thomas' family considered organ donation." If rigor mortis had set in, of course, organ donation would no longer be a possibility. Furthermore, one line in the story is significant but easy to overlook: "An attempt was made to lower her body temperature."[57] This should raise red flags since therapeutic hypothermia is induced when a patient suffers cardiac arrest, which is precisely why this woman was hospitalized in the first place. However, it has a confounding effect on the determination of brain death.

Commenting on these types of situations in a 2012 editorial, the coeditors in chief of the *American Journal of Critical Care* cautioned that "using phrases such as 'nearly brain dead' or 'almost brain dead' is never appropriate." They also point out that physician training must emphasize that "it is basically impossible to 'un-say' things once they're said."[58] Choosing words carefully

---

57. Hilary White, "Woman's Waking after Brain Death Raises Many Questions about Organ Donation," *LifeSite News*, May 27, 2008, https://www.lifesitenews.com.

58. Richard H. Savel and Cindy L. Munro, "Awakening (Mis)conceptions about Brain Death," *American Journal of Critical Care* 21.6 (November 2012): 379, doi: 10.4037 /ajcc2012459.

cannot be underestimated, given the difficulty that many experience in coming to terms with the complexities of brain death.

Imprecise media references to "brain death" are common. Therefore, it is not surprising that the general public lacks a solid understanding of it. For example, in 62 percent of the articles published in 2005 by the *New York Times* that mentioned brain death, "it was discussed incorrectly or misleadingly, causing readers to conclude that a brain dead person remained alive."[59]

An April 2013 study published in the *Journal of Medical Ethics* attempted to evaluate the extent and nature of this imprecision and to identify the specific areas of confusion. Canadian researchers collected 940 stories pertaining to brain death from leading print publications in the United States and Canada between 2005 and 2009. Their analysis revealed several items of interest. Close to 39 percent of the articles used the term *brain death* in a colloquial rather than a medical sense, that is, to refer to "a person or an action considered rash or thoughtless." These stories pertained to other spheres of life, such as politics, sports, art, and entertainment.[60]

Close to 47 percent of the articles mentioned brain death in relation to other medical and end-of-life issues,

59. James L. Bernat, "Theresa Schiavo's Tragedy and Ours, Too," *Neurology* 71.13 (September 2008): 965, doi: 10.1212/01.wnl.0000324281.33381.15.

60. Ariane Daoust and Eric Racine, "Depictions of 'Brain Death' in the Media: Medical and Ethical Implications," *Journal of Medical Ethics* 40.4 (April 2014): 255, doi: 10.1136/medethics-2012-101260.

and 11 percent of the articles referred to it simply as a medical diagnosis without providing any further details or context. Very few of the articles—2.7 percent in the United States and 3.6 percent in Canada—offered any definition of brain death. A similarly miniscule proportion of the articles specified the kinds of tests and conditions that need to be met to determine death on the basis of either the cardio-circulatory or neurological criteria, although 20 percent of the articles did discuss the determination of death in general. Another notable finding of concern was that "several articles suggested that the patient whose death is declared following the neurological criterion actually dies a second time when the heart stops beating. Some suggested that death occurred after organs were harvested for transplant."[61]

In many respects, this seems to mirror a common view held by the general public or, at least, those who have had to confront such a tragic situation. However, it seems more plausible that loved ones feel that death really occurred after the heart stopped beating, rather than that death occurred twice. Based on the considerable confusion about brain death apparent in the media, the authors conclude that "it is unclear whether the public considers [death by neurological criteria] as the straightforward equivalent of death."[62]

Tragic cases of brain death that involve a silver lining are also subject to the same type of misunderstanding. For example, a Canadian woman was declared brain dead in December 2013 when she was twenty-two weeks

61. Ibid., 255, 256.
62. Ibid., 257.

pregnant. In an attempt to bring the developing fetus to viability, artificial support was maintained, and in February 2014, a healthy boy was born. This is a remarkable feat of modern technology, although it remains an uncommon occurrence. Confusion about how the body of a dead patient can be maintained, much less how a child can be delivered under the circumstances, is not surprising: "Doctors told Benson that Iver's birth would be followed by his wife's death, since they would disconnect her from life-support. It is not known at this time if Robyn died as a result of the birth, or if her death was hastened by the removal of life support."[63]

Key Lessons

These cases are not exhaustive, but they are instructive for several reasons. The occurrence of errors reinforces the need for physicians to remain vigilant. In particular, making sure all the prerequisites are met and accounting for confounders are as essential as conducting a proper clinical examination and perhaps more challenging. Good communication between health care providers and families is critical; pressing for organ donation may understandably provoke resentment or suspicion. More precise reporting in the media would also improve public understanding of brain death in contradistinction to severe brain injury. Room for improvement is evident, yet despite these

63. Peter Baklinski, "'She Will Live on Forever within Iver': Canadian 'Brain Dead' Woman Gives Birth to Healthy Son," *LifeSite News*, February 11, 2014, http://www.lifesitenews.com.

reported lapses, no case has invalidated the concept of brain death.

Nevertheless, it can be challenging to regard as dead a pregnant woman whose body can be maintained long enough to deliver a baby. Similarly, it can be difficult to accept that a girl is dead when her body is undergoing changes consistent with adolescent development. Some have rejected brain death outright irrespective of these cases, while others have long regarded it as useful but nevertheless fictitious. Meanwhile, some in the Catholic tradition, who might otherwise be inclined to accept brain death, distance themselves from it to varying degrees on account of these complexities. Therefore, coherent reasons are needed to justify brain death. These reasons must be grounded in medical science and be compatible with the transcendent metaphysical proposition that man comprises the union of body and spiritual soul. It is to this philosophical discussion that we now turn.

5

Philosophical Justification for Brain Death

Error, abuse, and the variability that pervades the institutional protocols used to determine death raise the specter of routine deviation, which may call into question any blanket assurances of accuracy with death determination in actual practice. But error or substandard adherence to guidelines cannot directly disprove (nor can perfect adherence to guidelines substantiate) the validity of brain death. They cannot decisively inform, much less resolve, the separate ontological question of whether the concept of determining death by the neurological criteria is legitimate.

Lingering Opposition

There has been lingering and resurgent philosophical opposition to the concept of brain death even in Catholic intellectual circles. At the present time, objections tend to fall into two broad categories: (1) some brain-dead bodies exhibit prolonged somatic functioning, and (2) in some cases, patients declared brain dead may not satisfy the condition that *all* brain function has been lost.

Advances in the intensive care unit (ICU) largely account for the first category. In the early decades of brain death, it was not possible, as it is now, to sustain a brain-dead body for an extended period of time. D. Alan Shewmon, a pediatric neurosurgeon at the University of California, Los Angeles, is the foremost critic of brain death. He regards ongoing, complex somatic functioning as incompatible with death. His argument has garnered support from several quarters, but it has also prompted sharper defenses of brain death. The second category does reflect a bit of a dichotomy between the law as it is written—indeed, any language referring to the loss of *all* brain function—and the medical understanding of what constitutes brain death. The whole-brain-death standard as understood by the medical authorities does not require that literally all activity ceases or every neuron be destroyed, but it does require very specific and comprehensive destruction and is thus readily distinguishable from cases of severe brain damage.

Nevertheless, these complications are not easy to account for in everyday language or in scholarly language for that matter. Indeed, they have led the British scholar David Albert Jones to contend that many Catholic intellectuals have lost faith in the concept of brain death. Some critics who do not disagree with the concept in principle have voiced concerns about the possibility of misdiagnosis. Others question whether it can be used safely in the context of organ transplantation. Still others feel there is enough reasonable doubt to question the validity of the neurological criteria.

Given the spectrum of divergent opinions held by Catholic scholars, Jones concludes that none of the various explanations provide "good grounds for the moral certainty about death needed for current transplant practice to be ethically acceptable." He therefore stands squarely with the skeptics of brain death, stating that "unless and until adequate grounds for the use of neurological criteria can be restored, current practice will merit the admonition given by John Paul II: … [a] 'furtive, but no less serious and real, form of euthanasia.'"[1]

Australian ethicist Nicholas Tonti-Filippini is adamant that the clinical criteria *alone* are an insufficient means of diagnosing death, so he urges the universal use of blood flow testing. Here he is in good company. James Bernat has also suggested that blood flow testing should be a required element of brain death determination, particularly if the examiner is inexperienced or if there are any doubts about the determination. He came to this conclusion because he was disturbed by the multiple published accounts of the "alarming frequency of physician variations and errors in performing brain death tests, despite clear guidelines."[2]

---

1. David Albert Jones, "Loss of Faith in Brain Death: Catholic Controversy over the Determination of Death by Neurological Criteria," *Clinical Ethics* 7.3 (September 2012): 133, 139, doi: 10.1258/ce.2012.012m07, citing John Paul II, *Evangelium vitae* (March 25, 1995), n. 15.

2. James L. Bernat, "The Whole-Brain Concept of Death Remains Optimum Public Policy," *Journal of Law, Medicine and Ethics* 34.1 (March 2006): 40, doi: 10.1111/j.1748 -720X.2006.00006.x.

Patrick Lee and Germain Grisez feel that Shewmon has demonstrated the inadequacy of the usual argument in support of brain death even as they judge his case against it to be unsound as well. They maintain that brain death remains valid but propose a new interpretation, namely, that brain-dead patients have lost the radical capacity for sentience. They view the patient after brain death to be a living entity but not a human being—no longer a rational animal:

> Since a human being is a rational animal, anything that entirely lacks the capacity for rational functioning is not a human being. Since rational functioning in an animal presupposes sentient functioning, anything that entirely lacks the capacity for sentient functioning also lacks the capacity for rational functioning and so is not a human being. Since the human being is a mammal, a brain, or the capacity to develop a brain, is necessary for its capacity for sentient functioning. Therefore, any entity that entirely lacks a brain and the capacity to develop a brain is not a human being.[3]

This analysis is particularly noteworthy because it represents a reversal of sorts on Grisez's part from his earlier, influential defense of the whole-brain standard. John Finnis also expresses reservations while still concurring with the theoretical premises of Grisez's original defense of brain death: "Facts unknown to or unconsidered by Grisez and Boyle in 1978 seem to make it clear

---

3. Patrick Lee and Germain Grisez, "Total Brain Death: A Reply to Alan Shewmon," *Bioethics* 26.5 (June 2012): 277–278, doi: 10.1111/j.1467-8519.2010.01846.x.

that one can have dynamic, organic integration of the body without the contribution of the brain."[4]

However, Finnis's conclusion that "the brain is not demonstrably, and perhaps demonstrably is not, the necessary source of organic integration in even the post-embryonic human individual" seems to miss the mark because it does not distinguish between a spontaneous, naturally occurring source of integration and an external, technically delivered source of integration.[5] In living human beings, who by definition possess spontaneous integration, the brain is essential, whereas in the ICU, the brain is not needed to maintain somatic functioning. At any rate, the overwhelming majority of neurologists contend that the brain is the indispensible and chief integrator.

Patrick Lee and Robert George comment briefly on this topic in *Body–Self Dualism in Contemporary Ethics and Politics*: "Shewmon has presented a strong case. Nevertheless, since (it seems) the majority of neurologists are still not convinced that an individual can actually survive (or actually has survived) brain death, we ourselves are not certain which side is correct."[6] This rather neutral position is noteworthy since George was a member of the President's Council on Bioethics (PCBE)

---

4. John Finnis, "Brain Death and Peter Singer," in *Collected Essays*, vol. 2, *Intention and Identity* (Oxford, UK: Oxford University Press, 2011), 308–309.

5. Ibid., 309.

6. Patrick Lee and Robert P. George, *Body–Self Dualism in Contemporary Ethics and Politics* (Cambridge, UK: Cambridge University Press, 2008), 167–168.

and did not dissent from its conclusion that brain death is death. Lee and George contend that the definition of death is sound, even if the whole-brain criterion turns out to be mistaken. However, they maintain that changing the definition of death to allow for some type of higher-brain standard is unwarranted.

E. Christian Brugger also expresses reservations about the neurological criteria, particularly in light of the novel rationale the PCBE offered for it (which will be discussed later in this chapter). His case for "somatic *dis*-organization" as the definitive indicator of "organismic death" does seem similar to Shewmon's approach, at least in certain respects: "Current evidence provides 'sufficient grounds' for doubting they are always dead. Until these reasonable doubts are removed, an ethically justified caution requires that we should treat them as living human beings."[7]

Despite important concerns, there still is a solid philosophical rationale for accepting the legitimacy of brain death. This rests largely on the view held by St. Thomas Aquinas and espoused today by philosophers such as Jason Eberl that human death entails the loss of all the capacities (intellective, sensitive, and vegetative) of the spiritual soul and ultimately occurs only when the spiritual soul becomes unable to actively manifest or actualize its vegetative capacities under its own power.[8]

---

7. E. Christian Brugger, "D. Alan Shewmon and the PCBE's White Paper on Brain Death: Are Brain-Dead Patients Dead?," *Journal of Medicine and Philosophy* 38.2 (April 2013): 215, doi: 10.1093/jmp/jht009.

8. Jason T. Eberl, "A Thomistic Understanding of Human Death," *Bioethics* 19.1 (February 2005): 33, 39, doi: 10.1111/j.1467-8519.2005.00423.x.

Even if someone does not appear able to exercise any of his intellectual powers or to retain his sensitive capabilities, he is not dead if he is still able to exercise his vegetative functions *on his own*. On the other hand, once someone is irreversibly unable to do so, death becomes evident. The phenomenon of persistent somatic functioning among brain-dead patients in the ICU indicates that the soma can function in a *reactive* manner, but this is not a manifestation of the active functional capacities of the spiritual soul.

Anima Forma Corporis

When we speak of death, when we say that someone has died, what do we mean? Is it that the body has died? This is problematic because a human being comprises a body but is not only a body. Do we say that the person has died? This too is problematic because concepts of personhood can be subjective and can fail to correspond with biological reality. A person with severe brain damage, some claim, should be considered dead by virtue of lost personhood even though spontaneous vital functions remain intact. Conversely, it would be problematic to require the absence of all evidence of life in organ systems or at the cellular level. Such a determination would entail an impractical, invasive, and protracted process. Death, it is true, is a fundamentally biological phenomenon, as authoritative medical practitioners assert. But man is also a spiritual being endowed with a rational soul. So his death is also a spiritual event. The task is to identify as accurately as possible when that singular event takes place.

In the classical Catholic anthropological vision, death refers to the separation of the soul from the body. This definition was formally established at the Council of

Vienne in 1312. Generally speaking, it also corresponds philosophically with how the ancient Greeks, particularly Plato and Aristotle, viewed death. Man dies when the union of body and soul no longer exists, when the matter and spirit that were joined together become decisively separated. Only this type of broadly Aristotelian-Thomistic hylomorphic account of death is admissible in the eyes of the Catholic Church. Despite important distinctions, there is a great symmetry between the Classical and Catholic traditions. Both view the soul as the form of the body (*anima forma corporis*), or its animating principle.

The soul, according to Aristotle, is the cause of man's being, and as such, it is the primary act of bodily life. Furthermore, it first receives its being, which it then communicates to the body.[9] However, "it is not the soul which is the 'real man,' but the existential configuration, the unity of soul and body."[10] Similarly, the Church holds that "it is because of its spiritual soul that the body made of matter becomes a living, human body; spirit and matter, in man, are not two natures united, but rather their union forms a single nature."[11]

---

9. Marcelo Sánchez Sorondo, interviewed in "Questions for Neurologists and Others," in *The Signs of Death: The Proceedings of the Working Group—11–12 September 2006, Scripta Varia* 110 (Vatican City: Pontifical Academy of Sciences, 2007), xlvi.

10. Josef Pieper, *Death and Immortality*, trans. Richard and Clara Winston (South Bend, IN: St. Augustine's Press, 2000), 30.

11. *Catechism*, n. 365.

Aristotle noticed that the soul's capacities do not all emerge at the same time. With respect to embryogenesis and subsequent human development, he maintained that a vegetative soul and its corresponding capacities emerge first, followed by a sensitive soul and its corresponding capacities, and finally by a rational soul and its corresponding capacities. St. Albert the Great subscribed to this notion of a succession of souls and concluded that when the rational, or fully spiritual, form arrives, it absorbs and subsumes the previous forms. Aquinas, on the other hand, "requires the advent of the spiritual soul prior to the formation of the organism." He recognized that "if there were more than one soul there would be more than one form and thus more than one entity within the same individual–man."[12] Therefore, the spiritual soul does not absorb a separate vegetative soul and then a separate sensitive soul, but has within itself the capacity for such powers from its inception. A human being, formed by a single spiritual soul, remains the same single entity from conception to death.

Aquinas certainly did not hold that, at death, man loses in reverse a triumvirate of vegetative, sensitive, and rational souls that emerged sequentially at the beginning of life. Rather, once a living human organism is sufficiently developed, the rational soul becomes the form of the body and alone exercises control over all of these capacities. *Rational soul* does not refer exclusively to the powers of rational thought. The one soul has intellective, sensitive, and vegetative capacities. According

12. Elio Sgreccia, "Vegetative State and Brain Death: Philosophical and Ethical Issues from a Personalistic View," *NeuroRehabilitation* 19.4 (2004): 363.

to a Thomistic account of human death, all of the soul's capacities, including its vegetative ones, must be irreversibly lost to establish death. Indeed, Aquinas felt that death ultimately occurs only when the body becomes unable "to actualize the soul's vegetative capacities."[13] That is, even if someone does not appear able to exercise any of his intellectual powers or to retain his sensitive capabilities, he is not dead if he still can exercise his vegetative functions on his own.

Death is that state in which this animating life principle ceases to be present. Only the matter, now taking the form of a corpse, remains: "By death the soul is separated from the body, but in the resurrection God will give incorruptible life to our body, transformed by reunion with our soul."[14] The soul "does not perish when it separates from the body at death, and it will be reunited with the body at the final Resurrection."[15]

We may well be accustomed to conceiving of the soul as being immortal. This locution is found in the *Catechism of the Catholic Church*, and it is generally accepted as reflecting both the Christian position as well as the understanding of Plato. But greater precision may be helpful. The immaterial soul is part of man, and man is mortal. As Josef Pieper argues in *Death and Immortality*, "Strictly speaking, one should speak only of the *indestructibility* of the soul. For what is in truth

---

13. Eberl, "Thomistic Understanding of Human Death," 33. See also Jason T. Eberl, *Thomistic Principles and Bioethics* (New York: Routledge, 2006), 45.

14. *Catechism*, n. 1016.

15. Ibid., n. 366.

forever meant by this indestructibility is the immortality, exceeding all conception—not of the soul, but of the whole man." When Plato speaks of immortality he does not speak of the soul alone as if the soul were to be understood as the "real man." Consequently, even Plato "is no Platonist," because he "concedes that it is a catachrestic, inadequate use of language to call the soul immortal."[16]

Pieper also notes that this type of terminology (i.e., immortality of the soul) is not featured in the New Testament and that it is "strikingly absent from the great theological tradition." Aquinas instead uses terms such as *imperishability* and *incorruptibility* to refer to the soul.[17] This comports with the understanding of man as a composite of body and soul—not only the soul and not only the body. According to Aquinas, the soul "is not an entire man, and my soul is not I."[18] Writing in *Quaestiones disputatae de potentia Dei*, he advances the proposition that "the soul does not possess the perfection of its own nature except in union with the body."[19] He even states that "the soul united with the body is more

---

16. Pieper, *Death and Immortality*, 104, 105.

17. Ibid., 29.

18. Thomas Aquinas, *Commentary on the First Epistle to the Corinthians*, n. 924, available at https://dhspirory.org/.

19. Etienne Gilson, *History of Christian Philosophy in the Middle Ages* (New York: Random House, 1955), 361, cited in Pieper, *Death and Immortality*, 31.

like God than the soul separated from the body, because it possesses its nature more perfectly."[20]

In his commentary on St. Paul's First Letter to the Corinthians, Aquinas maintains that it would be difficult to accept the immortality of the soul while denying the resurrection of the body: "For it is clear that the soul is naturally united to the body and is departed from it, contrary to its nature and per accidens. Hence the soul devoid of its body is imperfect, as long as it is without the body."[21] In this vein, Pieper notes an intriguing parallel between Catholic belief and the thought of Plato, who "seems to be suggesting: If ever immortality is conferred upon us, not just the soul but the entire physical human being will in some inconceivable manner participate in the life of the gods; for in them alone is it made real its original perfection."[22]

From the considerations sketched above, a highly significant, overarching conclusion emerges: "It is not man's body nor his soul which 'dies,' but man himself." Pieper concludes that "the spiritual soul, although profoundly affected by death, connected with the body by its innermost nature and remaining related to it, nevertheless persists indestructibly and maintains itself, remains in being."[23]

Death properly corresponds to the man, not to the body or the soul. This must be kept in mind when

---

20. Thomas Aquinas, *Quaestiones disputatae de potentia Dei* 5.10.5, cited in Pieper, *Death and Immortality*, 32.

21. Aquinas, *Commentary on the First Epistle*, n. 924.

22. Pieper, *Death and Immortality*, 105.

23. Ibid., 27–28.

considering one of the chief objections to brain death, namely, that the death of the body does not necessarily ensue in the ICU once whole-brain death has been established. For instance, Jones specifies that the loss of confidence in brain death revolves around the question of whether satisfying the neurological criteria "necessarily demonstrates *the death of the body*."[24] This is a telling remark, since we should be interested in the death of the man, the human being, not the body.

In his important and often-cited statement about death, John Paul II wrote, "*The death of the person* is a single event, consisting in the total disintegration of that unitary and integrated whole that is the personal self."[25] Jones maintains that the philosophical premise John Paul II relied on to endorse whole-brain death was the "loss of capacity for somatic integration."[26] This is a recurring theme among those who feel that whole-brain death does not constitute death. For example, Nicanor Austriaco writes, "For the Pope, the absence of the soul is made manifest by the loss of bodily integration."[27] But it is important to underscore that John Paul II specified that the disintegration associated with death pertains to the *personal self*, which comprises body and soul; he did not strictly demand the disintegration of the body.

---

24. Jones, "Loss of Faith," 134, emphasis added.

25. John Paul II, Address to the eighteenth international congress of the Transplantation Society (August 29, 2000), n. 4.

26. Jones, "Loss of Faith," 135.

27. Nicanor Austriaco, "Is the Brain-Dead Patient *Really* Dead?," *Studia Moralia* 41 (2003): 303.

As will be discussed in more detail later, Aquinas argued that death occurs when material defects in the body become such that the matter is no longer able to support the form—when the material body is no longer suitable or properly disposed to sustain a rational soul. These material defects arise in the first place because the "pre-mortem human body is not *perfectly* informed by its rational soul."[28] The imperfect union of body and soul is consistent with the inevitability of death and perhaps even the colloquially and biologically informed expression that we are born, or programmed, to die.

Catholic Affirmation of Brain Death

The Catholic Church has methodically evaluated the issue of brain death by comparing the assessment of medical authorities with a sturdy philosophical anthropology. The Church's inquiries into the matter have spanned several decades and have consistently affirmed the legitimacy of the neurological criteria. Some pronouncements have been appropriately guarded, but none has cast aspersions on the legitimacy of the concept itself. The main concerns pertain to the rigorous application of the methodology used to determine death and, by extension, the inadmissibility of extracting vital organs from living donors.

In 1957, Pope Pius XII specified that doctors have the expertise "to give a clear and precise definition of 'death' and 'the moment of death' of a patient who passes away in a state of unconsciousness." The Pope noted that "the

---

28. Eberl, "Thomistic Understanding of Human Death," 32, original emphasis.

answer cannot be deduced from any religious and moral principle and, under this aspect, does not fall within the competence of the Church."[29] In 1981, the Pontifical Council Cor Unum stated, "The very most the Church could do would be to reiterate the conditions that would make it legitimate to accept the better judgment of those to whose specific competence has been entrusted [with] the determination of the moment of death."[30]

In 1985 and again in 1989, the Pontifical Academy of Sciences convened at the request of John Paul II to evaluate the concept of brain death. On both occasions, the academy judged that it is permissible to determine death by the irreversible loss of either brain function or cardiorespiratory function. The 1989 working group, echoing that of 1985, concluded, "A person is dead when there has been total and irreversible loss of all capacity for integrating and coordinating physical and mental functions of the body as a unit." Importantly, the council affirmed the validity of the neurological criteria "even if cardiac and respiratory functions which would have ceased have been maintained artificially."[31]

---

29. Pius XII, "The Prolongation of Life: An Address to an International Congress of Anesthesiologists November 24, 1957," reprinted in *National Catholic Bioethics Quarterly* 9.2 (Summer 2009): 330, 332.

30. Pontifical Council *Cor Unum*, *Questions of Ethics regarding the Fatally Ill and Dying* (June 27, 1981), n. 5.3.

31. "Final Considerations Formulated by the Scientific Participants," in *Working Group on the Determination of Brain Death and Its Relationship to Human Death: 10–14 December, 1989*, ed. R. J. White, H. Angstwurm, and

Such an understanding of death—centered on the utter lack of a patient's own *physical and mental* capacities—precludes any sort of dualistic conception whereby spontaneous vegetative functioning can be disregarded and death can be declared once it is supposed that all the higher functions of the brain are absent. But it also precludes a physical existence maintained solely by artificial means.

The patient in a persistent vegetative state, the patient with Alzheimer's disease, or the patient with dementia has not lost his "personal self." That is, the personal self who experiences death is not to be understood as consisting solely of characteristically human capacities such as identity, thought, volition, and memory. Rather, it refers to the living entity of the human being as an organismal whole, composed of body and soul, in which the body is capable of expressing *on its own* any of the capacities attributable to the spiritual soul that informs it.

Furthermore, because John Paul II did not demand proof other than the clinical evidence deemed necessary by the medical authorities, it seems reasonable to conclude that he was accepting the prevailing medical consensus, rather than demanding a more stringent criterion of his own, when he endorsed whole-brain death. Specifically, the Pope's view of the word *all* (as in all brain functions) would not differ from theirs. For example, when John Paul II specified that brain death is "considered the sign that the individual has lost its integrative capacity," inasmuch as it corresponds with

I. Carrasco de Paula (Vatican City: Pontifical Academy of Sciences, 1992), 81.

the "complete and irreversible cessation of all brain activity (in the cerebrum, cerebellum and brain stem)," he deferred to the medical understanding of whole-brain death. This is in contradistinction to both the slightly less stringent brain-stem standard adopted in some countries and the higher-brain death concept that some have advanced but the Church has steadfastly rejected.

In his 1989 address to the Pontifical Academy of Sciences, John Paul II asserted that "death can mean decomposition, disintegration, a separation. It occurs when the spiritual principle which ensures the unity of the individual can no longer exercise its functions in and upon the organism, whose elements, left to themselves, disintegrate."[32] This reasonably may be interpreted as not *requiring* actual somatic disintegration or decomposition in the ICU. The crucial specification is that the elements of the organism disintegrate when *left to themselves* following the separation of the soul from the body.

It seems abundantly clear that a brain-dead body does not and cannot direct any of its ongoing somatic functions. This is why the Church has deemed it reasonable to conclude that the soul is no longer present and why the medical concept of brain death does not seem to conflict with a sound Christian understanding of the human person.

There are no philosophical or scientific grounds for altering the conclusion John Paul II reached in 2000:

"Here it can be said that the criterion adopted in more recent times for ascertaining the fact of death, *namely*

32. John Paul II, "Discourse to the Participants of the Working Group," n. 4, in *Working Group on the Determination of Brain Death*, xxv.

> *the complete and irreversible cessation of all brain
> activity*, if rigorously applied, does not seem to conflict
> with the essential elements of a sound anthropology.
> Therefore a health-worker professionally responsible
> for ascertaining death *can use* these criteria in each
> individual case as the basis for arriving at that degree
> of assurance in ethical judgment which moral teach-
> ing describes as 'moral certainty.'"[33]

To judge that ongoing somatic functioning nullifies
this moral certainty seems unwarranted.

John Paul II's clear, if slightly reserved, endorsement
of brain death provides what is essential for practitioners
(and loved ones) facing such a wrenching situation: practical moral guidance. The required standard, it is worth
remembering, is moral rather than absolute certainty.
The Pope's statement, however, is not a *de fide* teaching;
it pertains, after all, to matters of science and medical
judgment. It is not irrevocable; should new, compelling
evidence arise, it could change. Nevertheless, the Church
has judged that brain death does seem to be compatible with a sound anthropology.[34] In fact, the summary
statement that emerged in 2006 from the latest round
of proceedings sponsored by the Pontifical Academy of

33. John Paul II, Address to the Transplantation Society,
n. 5, emphasis added.

34. For the history of the Church's deliberations pertaining to brain death, see John M. Haas, "Catholic Teaching
regarding the Legitimacy of the Neurological Criteria for
the Determination of Death," *National Catholic Bioethics Quarterly* 11.2 (Summer 2011): 279–299. "Thus three
times now, under two different pontificates, the Pontifical
Academy of Sciences has concluded that the neurological
criteria are a legitimate basis for determining death" (287).

Sciences tellingly is titled "Why the Concept of Brain Death Is Valid as a Definition of Death."[35]

Persistent Somatic Activity

Among some scholars, debate has persisted and even intensified of late primarily because some brain-dead bodies have exhibited prolonged somatic functioning. This phenomenon was initially surprising. In any case, it is not easy to dismiss out of hand. According to Shewmon, these cases shatter the validity of brain death. He presented his argument in an influential article that reviewed 175 cases involving the lack of asystole for at least one week following the determination of brain death.

In one exceptional case, a four-year old boy contracted meningitis and was subsequently determined to be brain-dead. When Shewmon conducted his review, the boy's body had been maintained for more than fourteen years. During that time, no spontaneous respiration or brain-stem reflexes were observed, and no intracranial blood flow was detected.[36] He was maintained in this state for approximately two decades.[37]

---

35. Antonio Battro et al., "Why the Concept of Brain Death Is Valid as a Definition of Death," in *Signs of Death*, xxi–xxix.

36. D. Alan Shewmon, "Chronic 'Brain Death': Meta-analysis and Conceptual Consequences," *Neurology* 51.6 (December 1998): 1538–1545, doi: 10.1212/WNL .51.6.1538.

37. Susan Repertinger et al., "Long Survival following Bacterial Meningitis–Associated Brain Destruction,"

One criticism of this article, aside from its under-emphasis of the rarity of such occurrences, was that the determination of death was not valid in all cases. That may well be the case; Shewmon's use of second-hand media accounts and the apparent holes in some of the primary records do raise questions.[38] Nonetheless, it is probable that some of these cases did involve prolonged somatic functioning in brain-dead bodies. At any rate, such occurrences are readily accepted as possible today. For example, Jahi McMath's body was maintained for over four years.

Several scholars, including respected Catholics, have reacted to such cases by concluding that brain death is not death, asserting that these cases raise sufficient doubt, or holding that the traditional rationale for death cannot be applied in such cases. This issue is particularly difficult because unlike other life issues, some formidable pro-life advocates have withheld their support from brain death if not rejected it outright. In general, disagreement would be inconceivable on matters such as contraception, abortion, and in vitro fertilization at the beginning of life or assisted suicide and euthanasia at the end of life. But brain death has divided otherwise natural allies. The central question is, does the persistence of somatic functioning in a patient clearly determined to be brain-dead nullify

Journal of Child Neurology 21.7 (July 2006): 591–595, doi: 10.2310/7010.2006.00137.

38. Eelco F. M. Wijdicks and James L. Bernat, comment on D. Alan Shewmon, "Chronic 'Brain Death': Meta-analysis and Conceptual Consequences," *Neurology* 53.6 (October 1999): 1369–1370, doi: 10.1212/WNL.53.6.1369.

the conclusion that such a patient no longer forms an unified, integrated whole comprising body and soul?

Duration

Importantly, the length of time a patient continues to exhibit artificially supported somatic activity after meeting the clinical criteria is immaterial to the coherence of brain death. Everyone declared brain-dead exhibits some measure of somatic functioning. If functioning *of that kind* necessarily indicates life, death could not be declared until it ceases. If it is not an indication of life, it has no bearing on the determination of death whether it can be sustained for a minute or for a decade.

The traditional emphasis on the impending cessation of all bodily functioning cannot be reconciled completely with this phenomenon. Consequently, accepting a declaration of brain death in the presence of persistent somatic activity might be perceived as shifting the goal posts rather than responding to developments in knowledge and understanding.

There is, however, an explanation for prolonged somatic coordination. Technical and pharmacological advances in the ICU enable the extended maintenance of heartbeat, circulation, and organ subsystems, which previously had been unsustainable. These cases typically require intensive monitoring and substitution measures to compensate for the lack of the brain's control over thermoregulation and cardiac and endocrine functions. Prior to the early 1980s, physicians could not maintain heartbeat and circulation for more than a week.[39]

39. James L. Bernat, "The Biophilosophical Basis of Whole-Brain Death," *Social Philosophy and Policy* 19.2 (July 2002): 340, doi: 10.1017/S0265052502192132.

Specifically, there was no way as there is now to compensate for "the loss of medullary control of circulation."[40] Today, practitioners commonly recognize that "contrary to previous perceptions that brain death invariably leads to cardiac arrest, any degree of brain failure, including brain death, can be sustained indefinitely with mechanical ventilation and vigilant care."[41]

Dependency

Dependency does not affect an organism's ontological status per se. Pius XII even specified that, in general, we should presume "that human life continues for as long as its vital functions—distinguished from the simple life of organs—manifest themselves spontaneously or even with the help of artificial processes."[42] Artificiality alone is not decisive; what is relevant, however, is "in *what manner* an organism is dependent upon certain types of artificial devices."[43] Brain-dead bodies do not

---

40. James L. Bernat, "A Conceptual Justification for Brain Death," *Hastings Center Report* 48 suppl 4 (November–December 2018): S19, doi: 10.1002/hast.946.

41. Sam D. Shemie, "Clarifying the Paradigm for the Ethics of Donation and Transplantation: Was 'Dead' Really So Clear before Organ Donation?," *Philosophy, Ethics, and Humanities in Medicine* 2 (August 24, 2007), 18, doi: 10.1186/1747-5341-2-18; and Steven Laureys, "Death, Unconsciousness and the Brain," *Nature Reviews Neuroscience* 6.11 (November 2005): 899–909, doi: 10.1038/nrn1789.

42. Pius XII, "Prolongation of Life," 332.

43. Jason T. Eberl, "Ontological Status of Whole-Brain-Dead Individuals," in *The Ethics of Organ Transplantation*,

direct or control ongoing somatic activity. On the contrary, continued functioning depends on the artificial oxygenation and circulation of blood. Therefore, it is not an assisted but still a naturally and spontaneously mediated condition.

Eberl draws a distinction between a ventilator and a pacemaker: the ventilator entirely takes over the function of breathing, which enables other parts of the body to function *in reaction* to this artificial input. This continues even after the ability to control somatic activity has been lost irreversibly, as is the case with brain-dead patients. A pacemaker differs in a fundamental respect because it *assists* cardiac function by helping to regulate it, but it does not entirely replace it.

But some obviously living persons are dependent on a ventilator, so that example cannot be the last word on artificial devices. Edmund Pelligrino makes this very point: "Patients with respiratory paralysis due to poliomyelitis or cervical spine trans-section have lived with the assistance of respirators for many years. Few would embalm or bury these supposed 'living cadavers' before their hearts had stopped beating."[44]

Persons suffering from these afflictions obviously are not brain-dead even though they cannot breathe on their own; they plainly manifest innate capacities of the soul despite the presence of crucial artificial intervention.

---

ed. Steven J. Jensen (Washington, DC: Catholic University of America Press, 2011), 56, original emphasis.

44. Edmund Pellegrino, "Personal Statement," in President's Council on Bioethics, *Controversies in the Determination of Death* (Washington, DC: PCBE, 2008), 110.

Technology can support circulation and respiration even in the absence of a patient's original heart or lungs, but artificial support simply cannot compensate for the loss of total brain function. As long as "the brain stem is still functioning, a person cannot be declared dead when circulatory and respiratory functions are continuing, even when they are functioning only because they are artificially supported."[45] Nevertheless, ongoing somatic functioning is a decidedly unsettling phenomenon and can be difficult to reconcile with death. Some of its features, particularly those related to ongoing indications of cardiac function, homeostasis, and pituitary function, are believed by some to challenge the concept of brain death.

Cardiac Function

As recently as the mid-2000s, many authoritative commentaries referenced the inherently precarious somatic condition of brain-dead patients, specifically that utter cardiac collapse was inevitable within a matter of hours or days after the loss of neurological activity. This observation implies that brain death is valid primarily because it invariably precedes cardiac death. However, as Allan Ropper observed, "If we are getting into the issue of whether cardiac function will eventually fail anyway, and that this justifies brain death, then we are at risk of creating an incorrect operational definition of brain death that depends on heart failure."[46]

---

45. Bernard Gert, "Definition of Death," *APA Newsletter on Philosophy and Medicine* 9.1 (Fall 2009): 7.

46. Allan H. Ropper, interviewed in "Questions for Neurologists and Others," lxxi; Eelco F. M. Wijdicks, interviewed

The prospect of cardiac arrest is a corroborative indication that the body has already lost the capacity to maintain its own integrated functioning. That fact has not changed even as ICU technology has advanced; there was always some amount of time after death was determined during which the patient could be maintained. We are now capable of doing so for longer periods of time.

Homeostasis

On the one hand, homeostasis is clearly a function of the brain, which suggests that its presence is incompatible with death. Yet there are clear indications that homeostasis can be maintained through technical intervention. In the proceedings of the Pontifical Academy of Sciences, Jerome Posner made this very point, emphasizing that the "homeostasis that is achieved requires intervention from the outside and thus is not a result of the organism as a whole demonstrating holistic properties." It is "not whole organism homeostasis."[47]

Furthermore, consider the following description of the characteristics of brain death, which distinguish it from serious but nonfatal neurological injuries: "Critical functions such as respiration and circulation, neuroendocrine and homeostatic regulation, and consciousness are permanently absent. The patient is apneic and

---

in "Questions for Neurologists and Others," lxix; and C. Pallis, "Whole-Brain Death Reconsidered: Physiological Facts and Philosophy," *Journal of Medical Ethics* 9.1 (March 1983): 32–37.

47. Jerome B. Posner, interviewed in "Questions for Neurologists and Others," xxxvii.

unreactive to environmental stimulation."[48] In brain death, respiration and circulation are considered to be innately absent even though these functions are induced and maintained artificially. After all, the brain-dead body is apneic and therefore utterly unable to breathe on its own. Likewise, the remaining neuroendocrine and homeostatic functions could not persist without artificially maintained circulation and other technical and pharmacological support. Consequently, homeostasis is maintained externally and is not a spontaneously occurring condition attributable to the patient.

Eelco Wijdicks offers the following assessment of how homeostasis may, at times, be sustained: "Salt and water homeostasis may be preserved initially in patients who do not have an acute mass severing the stalk. But in many others, progressive deterioration occurs because of profound polyuria and pulmonary edema, recurrent cardiac arrhythmias, intravascular coagulation, the need for increasing doses of dopamine, and possibly thyroid failure. This collapse distinguishes brain death from other comatose states."[49] The only function that cannot be artificially supported is consciousness; this is consistent with the fact that consciousness, or at any rate, thought, is not something that can be technically

---

48. C. Schnakers, "Clinical Assessment of Patients with Disorders of Consciousness," *Archives Italiennes de Biologie* 150 (2012): 36.

49. Eelco F. M. Wijdicks, author reply on "The Diagnosis of Brain Death," *New England Journal of Medicine* 345.8 (August 23, 2001): 617, doi: 10.1056 /NEJM200108233450813.

supported, produced, or maintained, precisely because it is a manifestation of the spiritual soul.

Pituitary Function

Some patients who satisfy the neurological criteria still exhibit functions associated with the hypothalamic-pituitary axis, such as hormone secretion. This would seem to indicate continued brain function. However, blood is supplied to the pituitary gland in part by extra-cranial circulation, for example, through the inferior hypophysial artery. Consequently, hormone levels do not necessarily decrease significantly after brain death. Similar processes have been observed in the pancreas, intestines, and adrenal glands.[50] Interestingly, even Shewmon acknowledges the legitimacy of this interpretation.[51] In essence, although some have claimed that laboratory evidence of persistent hypothalamic-pituitary activity is incompatible with death, it has not been widely

---

50. Ibid.; Leonard Baron et al., "Brief Review: History, Concept and Controversies in the Neurological Determination of Death," *Canadian Journal of Anesthesia* 53.6 (June 2006): 605, doi: 10.1007/BF03021852; Wijdicks and Bernat, comment on Shewmon, "Chronic 'Brain Death,'" 1369–1370; D. Alan Shewmon, author reply on "Chronic 'Brain Death': Meta-analysis and Conceptual Consequences," *Neurology* 53.6 (October 1999) 1371–1372, doi: 10.1212/WNL.53.6.1369; and D. Gardiner et. al., "International Perspective on the Diagnosis of Death," British *Journal of Anaesthesia* 108 suppl 1 (January 2012): i14–i28, doi: 10.1093/bja/aer397.

51. D. Alan Shewmon, "You Only Die Once: Why Brain Death Is Not the Death of a Human Being—A Reply to Nicholas Tonti-Filippini," *Communio* 39.3 (Fall 2012): 460.

interpreted as invalidating brain death, provided that the clinical examination is conclusive.

Nevertheless, further precautions may be in order, since it can be challenging to distinguish between relevant and irrelevant residual brain activity. Cases in which relevant brain activity persists would seem to signify that currently "accepted [brain death] tests are not sufficiently accurate to exclude false-positive [brain death] determinations" if, in fact, brain death was correctly determined, which cannot be known with certainty.[52]

Since "no one knows the precise minimum brain functions"[53] that are necessary for a living human organism to survive, Bernat contends that "the current tests for brain death may need to be tightened."[54] This would principally entail "requiring the absence of intracranial blood flow," since that stipulation would be preferable to the alternative of softening the current criterion. But no ancillary test is foolproof, some experts discount their importance altogether, and we may not currently "be able to confidently distinguish between zero and a tiny degree of blood flow."[55]

52. Anne L. Dalle Ave and James L. Bernat, "Inconsistencies between the Criterion and Tests for Brain Death," *Journal of Intensive Care Medicine*, e-pub June 21, 2018, doi: 10.1177/0885066618784268.

53. Ibid.

54. Bernat, "Conceptual Justification," S21.

55. Dalle Ave and Bernat, "Inconsistencies between the Criterion and Tests for Brain Death."

Reconciling Somatic Activity with Death

Reconciling these competing perspectives hinges on the acceptance of the majority view that whole-brain death is not strictly synonymous with the loss of every neuron, but rather corresponds with the loss of the critical capacities of the brain in its role of integrating the organism as a whole. Bernat maintains that the whole-brain formulation remains coherent even as he acknowledges its imperfections.[56] He credits others such as Shewmon for noting that the brain does not necessarily coordinate all somatic functioning and that other structures play relevant roles in bodily integration. For instance, in unusual cases, the spinal cord can maintain a tenuous homeostasis.[57] Acknowledging this fact, however, is a far cry from conceding that the roles of various parts of the body are essentially equivalent. This would imply that the parts are relatively independent rather than interdependent in specific ways, a concept that "is contradictory to the idea of an organism."[58]

The pertinence of this idea of an *organism as a whole*, understood as a higher, independently subsisting entity fundamentally distinct from the induced perpetuation of its components, cannot be overstated. Indeed, technological advances enabling the extended maintenance of somatic operations have led Bernat to regard this concept as the foremost justification for brain death because "the

---

56. Bernat, "Whole-Brain Concept of Death," 41.

57. Wijdicks, author reply on "Diagnosis of Brain Death," 617.

58. Georges M. M. Cottier, interviewed in "Questions for Neurologists and Others," xxxviii.

continued survival of many of its parts is fully compatible with the death of the organism."[59]

Coordination versus Integration

It is a mistake, as Melissa Moschella argues, to assign the same metaphysical status to every biological process. This, she surmises, is what those in Shewmon's camp essentially do: wrongly equate any degree of biological activity sustained through artificially maintained circulation with the soul itself:

> It seems that the concept 'constitutive integration' in Shewmon's argument effectively plays the role of the concept 'soul' in Aristotelian-Thomistic metaphysics. This is evident in his definition of constitutive integration as the type of integration that 'makes a body [simply] *to be* alive and *to be* a whole,' a definition equivalent to the Thomistic-Aristotelian definition of soul. Thus, to possess constitutive integration is to possess a soul, and therefore to be a unified whole.[60]

Yet the soul alone is the principle of *self*-integration, which requires the very thing Shewmon implicitly denies: *control* over one's essential vital functions. This is the fundamental metaphysical error at the root of the entire controversy, and it boils down to a failure to

---

59. Bernat, "Conceptual Justification," S19.

60. Melissa Moschella, "Deconstructing the Brain Disconnection–Brain Death Analogy and Clarifying the Rationale for the Neurological Criterion of Death," *Journal of Medicine and Philosophy* 41.3 (June 2016): 286, https://doi.org/10.1093/jmp/jhw006, citing Shewmon, "You Only Die Once," 435, original emphasis.

distinguish between *internal* and *external* principles of unity.

The truly amazing fact that some degree of functioning—even a great degree—can be induced and maintained by external causes (primarily the ventilator) does not therefore necessarily indicate the presence of the soul. The integration properly associated with a living human being must be *self*-integration. This in turn implies the metaphysical truth that an organism must "have an *internal* principle of unity, rather than a mere passive potentiality to be unified by external causes."[61]

In tandem with these metaphysical considerations, highly germane distinctions must be made in the realm of biology, principally, the differentiation posited by Maureen Condic between *coordination* and *integration*. To view the soul and bodily functioning as interchangeable, as Condic points out, fails to account for the profound difference between the parts and the sum, which leads to the conclusion that any degree of functioning constitutes the whole. But the whole is *more than* the sum of its parts. Ultimately, to regard the externally driven persisting functioning of the parts as tantamount to the whole "denies that any higher metaphysical or functional level is relevant to the consideration of death … [and] is fundamentally a reductionist argument that denies the existence of an integrated human whole beyond the properties of the cells and organs that comprise the body. If this view were correct, then

---

61. Moschella, "Deconstructing the Brain," 289, original emphasis.

human death would not occur until every single cell in the body had died."[62]

Explaining the persistence of somatic functioning following death, Condic notes that cells "retain their inherent, ordered properties that were established during life."[63] These "ordered relationships" enable extra- and intracellular chemical reactions to occur autonomously when oxygenated blood is circulated artificially. Since organs can function in isolation outside the body, it should not be surprising that they can function while perfused in a ventilated soma, their natural location.[64] Similarly, the cells in the body can remain alive for some time, much like they would in laboratory culture, provided that oxygen is artificially delivered. None of these activities rises to the level of integration we would rightly associate with a living being. So what persists is coordination rather than integration.[65]

The difference is one of *kind*, not merely one of degree. Coordination entails the "communication of parts in order to achieve an effective outcome," whereas integration denotes the incorporation of two

---

62. Maureen L. Condic, "Determination of Death: A Scientific Perspective on Biological Integration," *Journal of Medicine and Philosophy* 41.3 (June 2016): 269, 274, doi: 10.1093/jmp/jhw004.

63. Ibid., 272.

64. A. Battro et al., "Response to the Statement and Comments of Prof. Spaemann and Dr. Shewmon," in *Signs of Death*, 390.

65. Condic, "Determination of Death," 272–273.

or more elements yielding one single, unified whole.[66] The parts—cells, tissues, organs, and even larger sub-systems—can perform quite complex operations in coordination with one another but by themselves can-not sustain their own functions or remain alive without artificial intervention. By nature, they are at the service of the larger whole, the living organism, which "*globally* and *autonomously*" integrates all its activities in such a manner as to sustain the life of the organism as a whole.

In short, a coordinated biological response to specific signals is not equivalent to the integrated function char-acteristic of a living human being. For man, a rational animal, this entails mental function and "global, autono-mous integration of vital functions." The persistence of either is sufficient to indicate that a person is alive.[67]

Raphael Bonelli and colleagues likewise stress the distinction between "derived biological life" "and a living being." Derived life includes the simple life of cells, organs, and even remarkably, what they term the *heart-lung-compound*.[68] The reality of brain death as the death of the organism as a whole holds for all mammals once they have developed a brain, not only for man. With this common physiological understanding, they therefore maintain, the concept can be grasped

---

66. Ibid., 271.

67. Ibid., 264.

68. Raphael M. Bonelli, Enrique H. Prat, and Johannes Bonelli, "Philosophical Considerations on Brain Death and the Concept of the Organism as a Whole," *Psychiatria Danubina* 21.1 (2009): 4.

without explicit reference to the immaterial, spiritual soul of man.[69]

Eberl similarly argues that the entire debate over the whole-brain standard hinges on "the ontological and biological concept of an organism's 'integrative unity,'"[70] which he staunchly defends by equating it with the Aristotelian-Thomistic concept of "substantial unity." He stresses "that it is a body's loss of its soul's vegetative *capacities* that occasions the soul's separation." The death of a human being therefore rightly corresponds to the loss of capacity, "not just the cessation of the functions themselves."[71] Citing the absolute requirement of technological and pharmacological support in brain-dead bodies, Eberl observes that they lack the "active potentialities for vegetative, sensitive, and rational operations" characteristic of a body informed by the soul.[72] In an artificially maintained soma, we encounter only a passive, reactive potentiality.

The soul, as Aristotle understood it, confers the vital potencies on the matter of the body.[73] In brain death, the

---

69. J. Bonelli et al., "Brain Death: Understanding the Organism as a Whole," *Medecina e Morale* 3 (1999): 511.

70. Eberl, "Ontological Status of Whole-Brain-Dead Individuals," 44.

71. Eberl, *Thomistic Principles and Bioethics*, 51, original emphasis.

72. Ibid., 57; and Eberl, "Ontological Status of Whole-Brain-Dead Individuals," 58–59.

73. Stephen Napier, "Brain Death, Souls, and Integrated Functioning: Reply to Verheijde and Potts," *Christian Bioethics* 19.1 (April 2013): 25–39, doi: 10.1093/cb/cbt008.

body's remaining matter is no longer adequately organized to respond to the soul's life-animating promptings; the matter is still sufficiently composed, however,
to permit somatic functioning in a reactive manner.
Putting this concept into Thomistic terms, Eberl writes
that "when integrative unity has been irreversibly lost, a
body is no longer *proportionate* for rational ensoulment;
for it can no longer materially support a soul's proper
capacities in a *unified* substance." [74]

Eberl explains that such phenomena can, in Aristotelian-Thomistic terms, "be understood as emerging
from the interaction of a body's organ systems without
entailing that the body has the integrative unity required
for it to compose an individual substance that is *unum
simpliciter* with a single substantial form." [75] Johannes
Bonelli and colleagues also characterize the somatic
interactions occurring within a brain-dead body as
"reciprocal influences"; its parts are dependent upon
one another in a *reactive* manner. [76]

Self-Initiated Movement

A crucial aspect of integration is self-movement:

> We say that an animal lives when it begins to have
> movement from within itself; and we consider the
> animal to live as long as such movement is appar-
> ent in it. When, however, it does not have any
> movement from within itself, but is moved only
> by another, then the animal is said to be dead on

---

74. Eberl, "Thomistic Understanding of Human Death," 43.
75. Eberl, *Thomistic Principles and Bioethics*, 58.
76. Bonelli et al., "Brain Death," 506.

account of the failure of life. ... And thus living is said of all things that drive themselves to movement or operation to some degree; however, those things which by nature do not drive themselves to some movement or operation cannot be called living, unless by some degree of resemblance.[77]

Albert Moraczewski and J. Stuart Showalter emphasize that self-initiated *movement* (not to be understood strictly as movement in space) directed toward self-preservation and development is the fundamental characteristic of life: "Unlike inanimate objects such as a rock or a molecule, which are *acted upon*, an organism is a living entity that *acts (and reacts) from within*; it is self-initiated and acts in a manner directed to its preservation or enhancement, even if at times the external force may completely overwhelm it and kill or cripple it. Nonetheless, the basic mode of being is present."[78]

Stephen Napier uses similar terms, observing that the soul drives "the organization and development of the embryo's body from embryo to fetus, and from fetus to infant etc."[79] This is all consistent with Thomistic metaphysics, according to which a substance, such as a

---

77. Thomas Aquinas, *Summa theologiae* I.18.1, cited in Eberl, "Ontological Status of Whole-Brain Dead Individuals," 58.

78. Albert S. Moraczewski and J. Stuart Showalter, *Determination of Death: Theological, Medical, Ethical and Legal Issues* (St. Louis, MO: Catholic Health Association of the United States, 1982), 17, original emphasis.

79. Stephen Napier, "Brain Death: A Morally Legitimate Criteria for Determining Death?," *Linacre Quarterly* 76.1 (2009): 70, doi: 10.1179/002436309803889313.

human being composed of the composite of body and soul, is "able to exist *by itself* in that it possesses its own act of existing."[80]

In philosophical terms, natural substances and artifacts are distinct and often mutually exclusive entities. An artifact such as a ventilator cannot become a proper part of, or *incorporated* into, a natural substance such as a human being. Such an artifact cannot be informed by or inform a human being's substantial form: the soul.[81]

The person's inner drive and capacity to perform vital functions *on his own* correspond to the nature of the soul, which expresses its presence through the active exercise of its vegetative, sensitive, and intellective capacities. Where any such capacity is present, the soul is present, and where all such capacities are irretrievably lost, the soul is not. This, to clarify, is an inference we may reasonably and prudently make, not *direct* evidence of the soul's absence.[82]

The presence of externally driven somatic functioning cannot therefore be taken as a firm indication that the soul is present, whereas the irretrievable absence of the capacity for inner-directed functioning can be taken as a sign of the soul's absence. The question is whether somatic organization is a product of artificial, mechanized support or a reflection of that individual's very life

---

80. Philip Smith, "Brain Death: A Thomistic Appraisal," *Angelicum* 67 (1990): 6, original emphasis.

81. See Eberl, "Ontological Status of Whole-Brain-Dead Individuals," 56–58.

82. Napier, "Brain Death, Souls, and Integrated Functioning," 25–39.

principle. If it is determined to be wholly the result of the former, then strict physical disintegration, disorganization, or corruption is not required to establish death.

It should be noted that on the one hand, insufficient evidence that brain-dead bodies are living human beings does not constitute *proof* that they are not, but it can be counted as solid, compelling support. Yet on the other hand, we may safely—and importantly—conclude that the evidence of persistent somatic functioning is far from "a conclusive reason to reject the belief that brain death marks the loss of organismal integration."[83]

With limitations to our knowledge that leave us short of *proof*, Napier encapsulates the basis for arriving at a judgment with adequate confidence: "On the understanding that death is the soul's separation from the body, the absence of the body's own ability to integrate its vital functioning provides evidence sufficient for knowledge that the soul is no longer present. Since such ability is lost when a patient satisfies [whole brain–death critera, it] may serve as sufficient evidence for death."[84]

Some have claimed that only a total lack of functioning truly indicates the absence of self-movement and therefore of life, in part by arguing that it follows from the "classical metaphysical axiom that the only way one can know what a thing is, is from how it acts, i.e., from how it functions."[85] But is the axiom *agere sequitur esse*

---

83. Condic, "Determination of Death," 266, 274.

84. Napier, "Brain Death, Souls, and Integrated Functioning," 38.

85. Austriaco, "Is the Brain-Dead Patient *Really* Dead?," 302.

(doing follows being) a decisive principle in the technically wrought condition of brain death? It does not seem so. The question we must zero in on with respect to a brain-dead body is, does it act at all, or is it acted upon?

In fact, this question is not quite precise enough either, because we are interested in the man not just the body. The short answer, anyhow, is that the body is acted upon and reacts in turn, but the man does not act. To ascertain what something is from how *it acts* implies an actor, which implies an animator—a soul. The soul's presence is always evident by virtue of the functions it animates and sustains on its own, by the integration and organismic wholeness it imparts.

This sequence, however, cannot be read backward; somatic functioning is not always indicative of the presence of the soul in the context of the ICU. The view that it can be read backward gets to the core of the crisis of interpretation Jones has outlined. The fact that the soul is "the principle of bodily life," he writes, "can therefore be understood as implying that while the body is alive, the rational soul is present, even if the person cannot exercise the full range of human abilities."[86] This statement clearly conveys the pressing need to be on guard against stripping full moral status from living but vulnerable and dependent persons. But the patient unequivocally satisfying the neurological criteria for death can no longer exercise *any* of its own innate capacities. The problem, in essence, boils down to reaching an unwarranted

---

86. Jones, "Loss of Faith," 136.

metaphysical verdict based on the perpetuation of interactive biological phenomena.[87]

It is certainly commonsensical to look to the body for signs of life, and Jones is correct to reject the proposition that multiple deaths can exist: "The soul either is, or is not, informing the body."[88] But to conclude that, as long as there is bodily functioning, the soul is present and the person cannot be deemed dead with moral certainty, however, is to stop short of asking the chief question: What is driving the somatic functioning? If the source is innate, then we may rightly judge the soul to be present. However, if it is ultimately extrinsic, then we may not. The active functional capacity characteristic of a unified body and soul must be distinguished from the reactive capacity remaining within the body once it is separated from the soul.

The Brain as Integrating Organ

We must not lose sight of the fact that the soul alone is "the cause of the unity of a living being," and that "the soul is in *every part* of that being, and it is the source (as formal principle) of all that being's actions, operations and capacities."[89] In short, we must recognize the tension, which is not to say the conflict, captured in the second-century Letter to Diognetus: the soul is present

---

87. Moschella, "Deconstructing the Brain" 285.

88. Jones, "Loss of Faith," 138.

89. Moschella, "Deconstructing the Brain," 284, original emphasis.

in every part of the body and yet simultaneously remains distinct from it.[90]

The rational soul itself is the *formal cause* of the existence of the living, functioning, and unified human being: "It is in the soul, not in any particular body part or even in all of the body parts together, that the root capacity for organismal self-integration, as well as the root capacities for sentience and rationality, reside."[91] According to the classical Thomistic understanding, the critical distinction is that "the soul unites to the body as a *form* without an intermediary, but as a *motor* it does this through an intermediary."[92] The soul may operate through a material organ, but the union of body and soul is not mediated by any material organ; the soul, Aquinas taught, does not give existence by means of something else, since it is its source.[93]

Furthermore, while the soul is the formal principle of the body's own motion, "this does not preclude, however, one or more of the body's material parts or activities serving as a *secondary instrumental cause* of the soul's union with it. For such parts or activities may be necessary in effecting the body's disposition toward ensoulment—i.e., the well-ordered functioning of its

---

90. Letter to Diognetus (n. 5–6; Funk, 397–401).

91. Moschella, "Deconstructing the Brain," 290. See also Eberl, "Thomistic Defense of Whole-Brain Death," 236.

92. Thomas Aquinas, *Quaestiones disputate de anima* 9, cited in Battro et al., "Response to the Statement and Comments," 393, emphasis added.

93. See Aquinas, *Summa theologiae* I.76.7–8.

various organs: its *integration*."[94] Raphael Bonelli and colleagues note that the brain-dead body lacks a "central controlling part" that integrates reactive somatic activity into a "higher unit."[95] The preponderance of evidence points to the brain as this intermediary because it coordinates the physiological processes that maintain the body in a state that can be acted on by the promptings of the soul. At any rate, it is a truism established by the natural sciences that the brain is "indispensible for the biological existence of an individual," the only "necessary prerequisite of a living organism."[96]

Antonio Battro and colleagues make the important point that brain function is required for the "dynamic and operative physiological unity of the organism (over and above its role in consciousness), but not for the ontological unity of the organism, which is directly conferred by the soul without any mediation of the brain, as is demonstrated by the embryo."[97]

The reason we may feel comfortable accepting the death of the entire brain as the death of an individual is "not because the brain is the same as the mind or personhood, but because this intermediary of the soul in its dynamic and operative function (as a motor) within the body has been removed—'that disposition by which

---

94. Eberl, "Thomistic Defense of Whole-Brain Death," 237–238, original emphasis.

95. Bonelli et al., "Philosophical Considerations on Brain Death," 6.

96. Bonelli et al., "Brain Death," 511.

97. Battro et al., "Response to the Statement and Comments," 392–393.

the body is disposed for union with the soul.'"[98] Eberl puts this understanding of whole-brain death in similar terms, which is helpful because he carefully specifies that the brain is responsible for biological integration but correlated with, rather than equated with, rationality: "The cessation of *both* a brain's rationally correlated and biologically integrative functioning indicates a rational soul's departure as a particular human body's substantial form."[99]

In fact, the Pontifical Academy of Sciences also concluded that, at a biological and organic level, the "dynamic organic unity between the activity of the intellect, the senses, the brain and the body does not exclude but, on the contrary, postulates," as did Aquinas, "that there is an organ which has the role of directing, coordinating and integrating the activities of the whole body."[100]

In the academy's view, prominent critics of brain death display a "gross underestimation of the importance of the brain for the integrative function of the rest of the body."[101] The overwhelming medical consensus is that the brain does integrate the vital operations of the organism as a whole. Indeed, the dramatic manner in which the loss of brain stem functioning can be

---

98.   Ibid., 393, citing Aquinas, *Quaestiones disputate de anima* 9.

99.   Eberl, "Thomistic Understanding of Human Death," 45, original emphasis.

100. Battro et al., "Response to the Statement and Comments," 392.

101. Ibid., 391.

compensated for by an "elaborate scheme" of technical support (which, aside from the ventilator, includes blood pressure regulation, homeostatic support, and hormone replacement) seems to "reinforce as much as undermine the need for the central integration of the brain."[102]

Seen in this light, Grisez and Boyle's original argument from 1979 remains convincing; in fact, their characterization of ongoing somatic functioning is still relevant because, as they specify, the *source* of remaining integration in a brain-dead body is *mechanical* rather than innate: "If the functioning of the brain is the factor which principally integrates any organism which has a brain, then if that function is lost, what is left is no longer as a whole an *organic* unity. If the dynamic equilibrium of the remaining parts of the system is maintained, it nevertheless *as a whole* is a mechanical, not an organic system."[103]

Interestingly, the view of St. Augustine, which might be said to accommodate a less stringent, higher-brain standard, retains an uncanny relevance: "When 'the brain by which the body is governed fails,' the soul separates from the body: 'Thus, when the functions of the brain, which are, so to speak, at the service of the soul, cease completely because of some defect or perturbation—since the messengers of the sensations and

---

102. Eugene F. Diamond, "Brain-Based Determination of Death Revisited," *Linacre Quarterly* 65.4 (1998): 73, doi: 10.1080/00243639.1998.11878427.

103. Germain Grisez and Joseph M. Boyle Jr., *Life and Death with Liberty and Justice: A Contribution to the Euthanasia Debate* (Notre Dame, IN: University of Notre Dame Press, 1979), 77.

the agents of movement no longer act—it is as if the soul was no longer present and was not [in the body], and it has gone away.'"[104]

Incidentally, Aquinas and Aristotle believed that the heart was the primary organ through which the soul operated, but they did not equate the soul with that organ. Without the benefit of modern science, they were nonetheless connoting the valid concept that the soul worked through a primary organ in the process of integrating and directing the activities of the human organism as a whole.

These careful distinctions would seem to help remove some qualms, understandable as they may be, about the validity of brain death. All things considered, the case for the neurological criteria not only remains reasonable but strong. Indeed, in the midst of the ambiguities that seem to have heightened the controversy, Moschella is in good company (both medically and philosophically) in proposing that total brain death is not just a valid means of determining death, but ultimately the *only* one: it is the only way we can confidently conclude that "the material basis of the root capacities for self-integration and sentience have been lost."[105]

---

104. Augustine, *De Gen. ad lit.* 7.19 (Migne, PL 34.365), cited in Battro et al., "Why the Concept of Brain Death Is Valid as a Definition of Death," xxv. See also Nicholas Tonti-Filippini, "You Only Die Twice: Augustine, Aquinas, the Council of Vienne, and Death by the Brain Criterion," *Communio* 38.2 (Summer 2011): 310.

105. Moschella, "Deconstructing the Brain," 290.

Her use of the term *root capacity* parallels Eberl's use of *radical capacity*—both indicate that these capacities do not have to be immediately exercisable. Rationality is not omitted from her consideration, but given its immateriality, is not included in this formulation. Rather, she is homing in on the matter—the requisite material structures—that we may judge to be no longer proportionate, or suitable, to support the innate potencies of the soul. The maintenance of the soma through modern technology without the active participation of the brain does not obviate the physiological fact that the brain plays a primary role in sustaining, directing, and integrating the living human being's functions. Somatic maintenance, therefore, does not necessarily constitute evidence of authentic, self-driven integration. What matters is the source of the observable functioning. Seen in this light, criticism of the neurological criteria ultimately founders. Brain death is actually *the* gold standard, although some prominent bioethicists claim that the neurological criteria are no longer valid. Skeptics are even more misguided when they urge abolishing the dead donor rule to promote organ donation.[106]

Vital Work versus Integration

In 2008, the PCBE wrote a white paper titled *Controversies in the Determination of Death*, which provoked a flurry of reaction. The PCBE acknowledged the difficulties posed by cases of prolonged somatic functioning but maintained that the neurological criteria for determining death are still valid.

---

106. Ibid., 294 note 4.

The council reconciled these two positions by rejecting the traditional justification for equating brain death with human death, namely, the idea of organismal integration and what the PCBE called the "false assumption" that the brain integrates vital functions. The PCBE proposed an alternative explanation called "mode of being": an organism could still be recognized as a *whole* and therefore living organism if it persisted in "the fundamental vital *work* of a living organism—the work of self-preservation, achieved through the organism's need-driven commerce with the surrounding world."[107] If the capacity to perform fundamental vital work has been irreversibly destroyed, it is reasonable to conclude that death has occurred. Nevertheless, the PCBE concluded that the neurological criteria are sufficient to indicate that this has taken place.

From this perspective, an organism needs three fundamental capacities to carry on its vital work: "(1) Openness to the world, that is, receptivity to stimuli and signals from the surrounding environment. (2) The ability to act upon the world to obtain selectively what it needs. (3) The basic felt need that drives the organism to act as it must, to obtain what it needs and what its openness reveals to be available."[108]

Some members of the PCBE were not convinced that this was necessary; other observers were concerned about abandoning the integration-based rationale, because this has been the traditional justification

---

107. PCBE, *Controversies in the Determination of Death*, 60, original emphasis.

108. Ibid., 61.

accepted by the Church.[109] It is understandable that the move away from the concept of integration struck some as unsettling if not simply unfortunate. Much of the consternation seems to have stemmed from a conception that reduces integration to somatic functioning without reference to its provenance.[110]

Tonti-Filippini has been one of the more pronounced critics of the PCBE's justification, which he has deemed "opportunistic."[111] What concerns Tonti-Filippini most, however, is that neither Shewmon nor the PCBE uses "the concept of integration in relation to the doctrine of the soul forming or informing the body."[112] The crux of the matter, he notes insightfully, is that they use an

---

109. Nicholas Tonti-Filippini, "Has the Definition of Death Collapsed?," *Bioethics Research Notes* 21.4 (December 2009): 79–82.

110. There seems to be more immediately apparent consonance between traditional Catholic anthropology and the account of brain death put foward by the President's Commission in 1981. The commission argued that the primacy or centrality of the brain is due to "its overarching role as 'regulator' or 'integrator' of other bodily systems and the immediate and devastating consequences of its loss for the organism as a whole." President's Commission for the Study of Ethical Problems in Medicine and Biomedical and Behavioral Research, *Defining Death: A Report on the Medical, Legal and Ethical Issues in the Determination of Death* (Washington, DC: US Government Printing Office, 1981), 35.

111. Tonti-Filippini, "You Only Die Twice," 315.

112. Nicholas Tonti-Filippini, "'Bodily Integration': A Response to Robert Spaemann," *Communio* 39.3 (Fall 2012): 415.

altogether different concept of integration. Because the condition of *all* brain activity, strictly understood, may not be satisfied in patients with whole-brain death and because one reading of the concept of integration has been abandoned as its rationale by some authorities, Tonti-Filippini concludes, "As Catholics we can no longer rely on the secular application of the concept of death according to the notion that there is irreversible loss of all brain function. The secular medical standards would not seem to apply that definition strictly."[113]

There are, however, a number of elements in the PCBE formulation that parallel the findings of the Pontifical Academy of Sciences and seem to be compatible with sound Catholic anthropology.[114] For example, the academy agrees with the PCBE that technology is capable of *masking* the fact that death has occurred: "In reality, the ventilator and not the individual, artificially maintains the appearance of vitality of the body. Thus, in a condition of brain death, the so-called life of the parts of the body is 'artificial life' and not natural life. In essence, an artificial instrument has become the principal cause of such a non-natural 'life.' In this way, death is camouflaged or masked by the use of the artificial instrument."[115]

The Pontifical Academy of Sciences, noting that Aristotelian-Thomistic philosophy is incompatible

---

113. Tonti-Filippini, "You Only Die Twice," 322.

114. It is interesting to note that there were three Catholics on the PCBE, each of whom reached different conclusions.

115. Battro et al., "Why the Concept of Brain Death Is Valid as a Definition of Death," xxix.

with the possibility that the brain-dead body of a fully developed human being could be informed by a soul, reiterated the viewpoint that death can be camouflaged:

> The destruction of the brain (or the destruction of the brain cells) causes the body to lose the capacity or disposition to receive life, thus preventing the soul from giving life and being to the body. Therefore, what remains is not a body but a corpse, even when it may seem alive because a ventilator masks its death. It is not a human body because it neither has the being nor the life of the intellectual soul, but 'ex-sists' in time as a corpse, the inexorable decomposition process of which is slowed down and camouflaged by artificial instruments.[116]

The PCBE reached the same conclusion: "When a ventilator supports the body's vital functions, this technological intervention obscures our view of the phenomenon. What seem to be signs of continued life in an injured body are, in fact, misleading artifacts of the technological intervention and obstacles to ascertaining the truth."[117] The council emphasized the crucial relevance of an organism's own drive to breathe, which reflects its "own impulse, exercised on its own behalf, and [is] indispensable to its continued existence." Spontaneous breathing is an obvious sign of an organism's vital work even if consciousness is absent, whereas the "technologically supported, *passive condition of being*

---

116. Sánchez Sorondo, interviewed in "Questions for Neurologists and Others," xlvii.

117. PCBE, *Controversies in the Determination of Death*, 52.

ventilated" is not.[118] Although some critics regard the PCBE's emphasis on spontaneous breathing as arbitrary, there is a certain parallel to Aquinas, who as part of his account of death, maintained, "If breath is subtracted, the union of soul to body fails; not because breath is the medium [of the union], but because the disposition is removed through which the body is disposed toward this union."[119]

Likewise, the "integrated somatic functioning," which the PCBE judged to be incompatible with the traditional rationale for accepting brain death, is not equivalent to the kind of Aristotelian-Thomistic integrative unity the Church has traditionally recognized as the composite of body and soul. For instance, "what animates the motor act of spontaneous breathing, in open commerce with the surrounding air," the PCBE writes, "is the inner experience of need, manifesting itself as the drive to breathe."[120] A Catholic would finish the sentence simply by saying "is the soul." Spontaneous breathing is an important component and manifestation of the soul's own vegetative capacities. The very use of the verb *animate* is telling, as its root literally signifies the soul.

---

118. Ibid., 62, original emphasis.

119. Aquinas, *Summa theologiae* I.76.7 ad 2, cited in Eberl, "Thomistic Understanding of Human Death," 33.

120. PCBE, *Controversies in the Determination of Death*, 62. The authors are careful to specify that this drive to breathe cannot be the exclusive criteria. After all, some people need assistance breathing yet go on living.

Contributing to an assembly of the Pontifical Academy of Life almost a decade prior to the PCBE report, Corrado Manni defended the validity of whole-brain death using terms and concepts the PCBE would ultimately adopt, writing that the brain enables the organism to maintain "coordinated activities *oriented for its own preservation*"; the evidence for this is "*its interaction with the environment.*"[121]

The language is different, since the PCBE consciously attempts to frame its description without any theological reference point. Yet one could accept both explanations: the PCBE interpretation does not threaten the Catholic view, nor does accepting the Catholic view preclude crediting the PCBE construction. Both interpretations emphasize the person's inner drive or capacity to perform vital functions on one's own.

Eberl remains unconvinced that the arguments from critics like Shewmon are strong enough to eschew the integrative-unity rationale. He finds the PCBE analysis intriguing because it acknowledges and incorporates Shewmon's findings about persistent somatic functioning and still upholds the whole-brain standard. By his reading, it does not blow up the traditional rationale for accepting death. In fact, it "is certainly consistent with the concept of an organism's integrative unity and Aquinas's own understanding of 'life,' and thus provides

---

121. Corrado Manni, "A Report on Cerebral Death," in *Proceedings of Fifth Assembly of the Pontifical Academy for Life: The Dignity of the Dying Person* (Vatican City: Libreria Editrice Vaticana, 2000), 106, 114, emphasis added.

additional, not contrary support for the whole-brain standard."[122]

Ancillary Testing

The current evidence regarding ancillary tests also has relevant philosophical implications. In a certain sense, it seems fitting that ancillary tests cannot independently determine the ontological status of the patient. Interpreting the status of a patient by means of clinical functions rather than technically detected cellular life seems to correspond better with the reality that death marks the separation of the soul from the body (i.e., the hylomorphic account of death). We think of the soul *informing* the body, enabling it to function on its own as a unified whole; in death, the body clinically manifests that it is no longer able to support the vital potencies of the soul. We do not identify the soul with any particular isolated cellular life. Therefore, requiring a specific form of ancillary technology to establish that death has occurred in the context of a clear-cut clinical determination (e.g., by detecting some signs of neuronal activity or blood flow) would run the risk of equating any of those isolated phenomena as indicative of the presence of the soul.

---

122. Eberl, "Ontological Status of Whole-Brain-Dead Individuals," 58 note 48. Eberl argues that retaining integrative unity ultimately depends upon the capacity for *spontaneous* respiration and circulation: "Shewmon's case for abandoning the whole-brain criterion depends upon there being cases in which spontaneous heartbeat and respiration occur in the absence of whole-brain functioning, and he has not presented any such case" (61).

This is ironic because critics of whole-brain death often claim that its proponents equate the brain with the soul, which they correctly observe cannot be reduced or confined to any particular organ.[123] Yet suggesting that any particular imaging or technological test (again, supposing the clinical criteria are clearly met) should be decisive would seem to suggest that these technological tests are able to detect the presence or absence of the soul.

The appeal of a foolproof technological way to provide an irrefutable verdict is easy to understand. But are we to assume that what we see through an imaging technique necessarily corresponds to the presence or absence of the vital potencies attributable to the soul alone? Should this evidence supersede what is ascertainable through a careful clinical examination by which a patient manifests his physiological incapacities? That would seem a vastly more challenging proposition to defend philosophically and medically.

In light of the imprecision associated with terminology such as whole-brain death, which can occur alongside ongoing pituitary function and thermoregulation, one critic maintains that in recent years, "a growing consensus has developed among bioethicists and

---

123. Robert Spaemann, "Is Brain Death the Death of a Human Being?," *Humanum* 4.1 (2014): 5–14; and Monica Seeley, "Not Quite Dead? The Case for Caution in the Definition of 'Brain Death,'" *Catholic World Report* (February 1998): 48–55, available at https://www.catholiceducation .org/en/science/ethical-issues/not-quite-dead-the-case -for-caution-in-the-definition-of-brain-death.html.

philosophers that brain death is actually incoherent."[124] It must be said, however, that the consensus remains strong within the fields of neurology and medicine. This critic, it should also be noted, maintains that death itself eludes definition, and that the "deeply philosophically flawed" conceptual framework, which proponents of whole-brain death accept, cannot supply sufficient clarity to overcome death's inherent fuzziness.

However, the Aristotelian-Thomistic framework actually provides the most fitting and coherent account of human death even when it is ostensibly inconsistent with the loss, strictly speaking, of "all" brain activity. It provides a reasonable, as opposed to an arbitrary, explanation of why some activity does not constitute evidence of the integrative unity of body and soul. Scientific language is unsuited to precisely account for such discrepancies. So it seems fitting that there is a gap of meaning between the potentially ambiguous death of the *entire* brain and the reality of death. Even with such incongruence in some cases, the whole-brain death standard represents "the best contemporary interpretation of the Thomistic view of human death."[125]

This focus on organismic capacity rather than isolated cellular life in the brain also has an important logical symmetry to controversies surrounding the beginning of life. Critics of brain death sometimes point to the developing human embryo as evidence that a

---

124. Winston Chiong, "Brain Death without Definitions," *Hastings Center Report* 35.6 (November–December 2005): 20, emphasis added, doi: 10.1353/hcr.2005.0105.

125. Eberl, *Thomistic Principles and Bioethics*, 121.

brain is not required for human life. Conversely, others claim that an embryo does not have full moral status as a member of the human family, because it lacks a brain at that stage of development. But it is precisely the ability of the embryo to function as an organism under its own intrinsic power and proper to its stage of development that makes it a living being.

Drawing this parallel, Condic argues that "the ability to act as an integrated whole is the *only* function that departs from our bodies in the moment of death, and is therefore the defining characteristic of 'human life.'"[126] The objective nature of this definition makes it alone capable of standing up to other subjective considerations, which can easily be used to contest the living status of vulnerable human beings at the very beginning and very end of life. Although this assertion is compatible with the Thomistic view, it does not depend on any particular "religious belief or subjective judgment."

As noted earlier, a person with a functioning brain clearly remains alive even if respiration and circulation is artificially maintained. But the converse is not true: artificially maintained respiration and circulation do not constitute life in the context of complete brain destruction. Mechanically supplied cardiopulmonary function has been rendered "irrelevant to death, because heart and lung functioning has lost its special relationship with the organism."[127] This, in turn, ultimately lends

126. Maureen L. Condic, "Life: Defining the Beginning by the End," *First Things* (May 2003): 54, original emphasis.

127. James L. Bernat, "How Much of the Brain Must Die in Brain Death?," *Journal of Clinical Ethics* 3.1 (Spring 1992): 22.

itself to a brain-based, or neuro-centric, standard of death rather than one based on circulation.

There are those who feel that brain-dead patients cannot be categorically classified as living or dead. Shewmon contends that "a holistic level of integration does occur in *at least some* brain-dead bodies."[128] Therefore, some of these patients may indeed be dead while others may be alive. Suppose for a moment that this were true. On what basis could a clinician make the proper distinction on a case-by-case basis? It could not be based on the clinical examination, even one corroborated by ancillary tests, as long as somatic functioning persists.

Shewmon therefore posits that circulation, not the brain, is the *sine qua non* for life inasmuch as circulation is indispensable for somatic functioning. That, in turn, may be how to distinguish the "living" brain-dead from the "dead" brain-dead. Actual control over one's own circulation and respiration does not enter this picture, and is thus in readily apparent contrast with the view that the brain, inasmuch as it is responsible for controlling circulation and respiration, is the *sine qua non* for life because it is necessary for self integration.[129]

In an apparent attempt to assuage the standoff between competing camps, Shewmon has also proposed partitioning the concept of death such that two different deaths could be recognized: a social and legal civil death that precedes a metaphysical death. Civil death (passing away) he likens to birth (civil beginning), whereas

---

128. Shewmon, "You Only Die Once," 429, emphasis added.

129. Moschella, "Deconstructing the Brain," 291–292.

metaphysical death, which he labels *de-animation*, is akin to conception. This is an explicitly dualistic account, which he terms *hylomorphic dualism*.[130] There are obvious problems with settling on something other than ontological reality—whether at the beginning or the end of life—to judge whether an organism possesses full moral status. It is hard to see how a prior civil death could be legitimately recognized if he were correct about the ontological status of a patient who has passed away but is not yet de-animated.

Inadequacy of Higher-Brain Death

Advocates of higher-brain death disregard the significance of spontaneous vegetative functioning; some argue that if a person has lost the higher rational capacities, he should be considered dead because he has lost what Veatch ambiguously termed "that which is essentially significant to [human] nature."[131] Aquinas's

---

130. D. Alan Shewmon, "Constructing the Death Elephant: A Synthetic Paradigm Shift for the Definition, Criteria, and Tests for Death," *Journal of Medicine and Philosophy* 35.3 (June 2010): 256–298, https://doi.org/10.1093/jmp/jhq022.

131. Robert M. Veatch and Lainie F. Ross, *Transplantation Ethics*, 2nd ed. (Washington, DC: Georgetown University Press, 2015), 54. Elsewhere, Veatch equates "the end of a human person's biological existence ... [with] the loss of 'the capacity to think, feel, be conscious and aware of other people.'" Eberl, "Thomistic Understanding of Human Death," 34, citing Robert M. Veatch, "Whole-Brain, Neocortical, and Higher Bain Related Concepts," in *Philosophy and Medicine*, vol. 31, *Death: Beyond Whole-*

anthropology admits no dichotomy between person and body.[132] He would reject the conclusion that any such person's rational soul has departed and that the body—now *substantially* different—is formed not by a rational soul but by a sensitive or vegetative one. In other words, "the higher-brain account involves an unwarranted separation of a soul's rational capacities from its sensitive and vegetative capacities."[133]

Since the spiritual soul, or "animative principle," as Elio Sgreccia described it, is responsible for both higher functions and vegetative-sensitive capacities, it can be said to be present in any person with any of these capacities; one "must be considered alive, even when gravely and persistently hindered in the application of his/her cognitive functions."[134] Such patients, despite severe impairment, "retain enough functional integrity to be compatible with the human soul."[135]

Indeed, some of the most fascinating discoveries in recent neuroscience indicate that patients suffering from profound neocortical damage can have greater awareness and higher capacities than had typically been supposed, enabling us to refine our understanding of

---

Brain Criteria, ed. Richard M. Zaner (New York: Springer, 1988), 173.

132. Philip Smith, "Personhood and the Persistent Vegetative State," *Linacre Quarterly* 57.2 (May 1990): 51.

133. Eberl, "Thomistic Understanding of Human Death," 39.

134. Sgreccia, "Vegetative State and Brain Death," 361.

135. Smith, "Personhood and the Persistent Vegetative State," 57.

their condition. These patients do not form a monolithic cohort; there are gradations of severity within this spectrum of neurologic injury.

As a result of advances in our understanding, the terminology itself has been sharpened. The broad spectrum of severe neurological impairment is now being classified as disorders of consciousness. Within that spectrum, the vegetative state now is referred to as unresponsive wakefulness syndrome (UWS), which is different from the minimally conscious state (MCS).[136] Patients in the former category are, as the name implies, both unresponsive and wakeful; this new UWS designation altogether bypasses the term *vegetative*, which in everyday usage is associated with several inaccurate or ambiguous, if not always pejorative, connotations.[137] Patients in the latter condition exhibit, as the name implies, minimal but clearly discernable indications of consciousness; they display "behaviors that require at least periodic or fragmentary awareness."[138] Those in

---

136. Ralf J. Jox et al., "Disorders of Consciousness: Responding to Requests for Novel Diagnostic and Therapeutic Interventions," *Lancet Neurology* 11.8 (August 2012): 732, doi: 10.1016/S1474-4422(12)70154-0.

137. Steven Laureys et al., "Unresponsive Wakefulness Syndrome: A New Name for the Vegetative State or Apallic Syndrome," *BMC Medicine* 8 (November 1, 2010): 68, doi: 10.1186/1741-7015-8-68.

138. James L. Bernat, "Increasing Awareness in Unawareness," *JAMA Neurology* 70.10 (October 2013): 1231, doi: 10.1001/jamaneurol.2013.3746.

a MCS, incidentally, tend to have much more favorable outcomes than those in a UWS.[139]

Distinguishing between these two states is challenging; the rate of misdiagnosis can be as high as 40 percent.[140] In fact, MCS occurs much more frequently than the vegetative state or UWS, and "false-positive diagnostic error for [the vegetative state] remains disturbingly high."[141] A review published in 2009 found that the rate of misdiagnosis of the vegetative state by and large had not changed in the preceding fifteen years.[142]

Some patients in these categories can have greater cognitive capacities and awareness of their surroundings than previously presumed even though their "clinical examinations suggests otherwise."[143] They cannot, however, demonstrate these higher capacities through outward behavior. A fascinating 2013 study published in *JAMA Neurology* demonstrated the effectiveness of a brain scanning technique (fMRI) in detecting not only conscious awareness but even the capacity to

---

139. Caroline Schnakers et al., "Diagnostic Accuracy of the Vegetative and Minimally Conscious State: Clinical Consensus versus Standardized Neurobehavioral Assessment," *BMC Neurology* 9 (July 21, 2009). 35, doi: 10.1186/1471-2377-9-35.

140. Jox et al., "Disorders of Consciousness," 732.

141. Bernat, "Increasing Awareness," 1231.

142. Schnakers et al., "Diagnostic Accuracy of the Vegetative and Minimally Conscious State."

143. Jox et al., "Disorders of Consciousness," 732.

communicate in some patients who were otherwise nonresponsive.[144]

This novel study demonstrates that patients in either UWS or MCS can communicate by selectively paying attention to auditory commands. This finding adds another dramatic dimension to knowledge gained from previous studies, which demonstrated that such patients could respond to commands by modulating brain activity rather than through speech or movement. Researchers were able to detect acts of intention and thereby erase any doubt that such a patient is aware of self and surroundings.[145]

Other research has discovered remarkable indications of subjective emotional experiences in these patients. One study published in 2013 used fMRI to compare four patients in the vegetative state with thirteen healthy controls. Participants were shown pictures of unfamiliar faces, familiar faces, and themselves. Separately, they were also asked to actively imagine one of their parents' faces. On the basis of the nature and type of robust brain activity observed in both patients and controls, the researchers concluded that the cognitive processing exhibited by patients in a persistent vegetative state indicates "the ability for covert emotional

---

144. Lorina Naci and Adrian M. Owen, "Making Every Word Count for Nonresponsive Patients," *JAMA Neurology* 70.10 (October 2013): 1235–1241, doi: 10.1001/jama neurol.2013.3686.

145. Adrian M. Owen et al., "Detecting Awareness in the Vegetative State," *Science* 313.5792 (September 8, 2006): 1402, doi: 10.1126/science.1130197.

awareness of self and the environment."[146] These states of awareness may well be transient, they cautioned, and the overall nature and extent of such emotional experience is naturally a matter of some debate. We may nonetheless conclude that such patients possess not only autonomic vegetative functions, which defenders of whole-brain death take as unequivocally sufficient signs of life, but that they may also possess some of those distinctly human capacities that advocates of the higher-brain formulation thought had been absolutely destroyed.

Indeed, researchers at the University of Liège, in Belgium, documented another short-term advance in the treatment of those in a MCS: a simple, non-invasive form of electric stimulation called transcranial direct-current stimulation can temporarily but systematically improve signs of conscious awareness and respon-siveness. Improvement was reported in 43 percent of patients in a MCS.[147] This form of therapy was effective even on those who had been in a MCS for several years; unfortunately, the same results were not observed for those in a UWS.

Cognitive and motor impairment is still severe in these patients. Arguments will probably continue to be made that such persons should not be considered

---

146. Haggai Sharon et al., "Emotional Processing of Personally Familiar Faces in the Vegetative State," *PLoS ONE* 8.9 (September 25, 2013), e74711, doi: 10.1371 /journal.pone.0074711.

147. Aurore Thibaut et al., "tDCS in Patients with Dis-orders of Consciousness: Sham-Controlled Randomized Double-Blind Study," *Neurology* 82.13 (April 1, 2014): 1112–1118, doi: 10.1212/WNL.0000000000000260.

alive or, at least, that it is permissible to extract their organs anyway. In fact, notoriously utilitarian authors such as Julian Savulescu go to some length to downplay the ethical significance of "transitory and fluctuating consciousness," since it does not confer full moral status to the patient: "Paradoxically, the discovery of consciousness in very severely brain-damaged patients may provide more reason to let them die."[148] What matters, in his view, is whether patients have "the right kinds of sophisticated mental states that underlie full moral status."[149] Denying full moral status to a living human being is obviously foreign to Catholic tradition and prevailing medical norms.

It may well be true that in certain respects, the distinction between UWS and MCS may not greatly influence treatment-related decision making. It is not known how establishing awareness in a patient affects family members or other decision makers; for instance, "if a patient is shown to be aware, do family members speak to and handle the patient differently?"[150] That seems eminently likely; nevertheless, in all such trying cases, ordinary means of support should be provided

---

148. D. J. Wilkinson et al., "Functional Neuroimaging and Withdrawal of Life-Sustaining Treatment from Vegetative Patients," *Journal of Medical Ethics* 35.8 (August 2009): 508, doi: 10.1136/jme.2008.029165.

149. Neil Levy and Julian Savulescu, "Moral Significance of Phenomenal Consciousness," in *Progress in Brain Research*, vol. 177, *Coma Science: Clinical and Ethical Implications*, ed. Steven Laureys, Nicholas D. Schiff, and Adrian M. Owen (Amsterdam: Elsevier, 2009), 368.

150. Jox et al., "Disorders of Consciousness," 735.

regardless of the level of the patient's consciousness. But to anyone seriously contesting whether these patients are, in fact, alive, these types of findings should represent the death knell to that higher-brain death line of reasoning.

That, however, does not mean that some organ-transplantation enthusiasts would not be content simply to circumvent the dead donor rule altogether. In fact, there are indications of popular support for disregarding the dead donor rule even when the distinction between brain death and the vegetative state is made explicitly clear. A survey published in the *Journal of Medical Ethics* found that 71 percent of respondents actually were in favor of dispensing with the dead donor rule for a patient in a vegetative state even if the act of organ donation were to cause the death of the donor.[151]

The Ultimate Standard of Death

The preceding findings on the capacities of some patients in a vegetative state, compelling as they are, do not have any bearing on the separate classification of brain death. However, they reinforce and validate the distinction between brain death and other forms of severe neurological trauma. To boil it down, the

---

151. Michael Nair-Collins, Sydney R. Green, and Angelina R. Sutin, "Abandoning the Dead Donor Rule? A National Survey of Public Views on Death and Organ Donation," *Journal of Medical Ethics* 41.4 (April 2015): 297, doi: 10.1136/medethics-2014-102229.

difference is "between a severely impaired brain function and the complete absence of it."[152]

This distinction is not arbitrary, but it is reflection of different underlying realities. It is not a utilitarian fabrication. It is not Cartesian disregard for anything but higher-brain function. From a medical point of view, the distinction is reasonable, coherent, and well grounded; when conditions permit a clinical examination for brain death and it is conducted properly, there is no diagnostic error. As Philip Smith described the persuasiveness of the available evidence, "The validity of the criteria must be considered to have been established with as much certainty as is possible in biology or medicine."[153]

Whole-brain death represents a convergence between medicine and physiology, on the one hand, and classical philosophical anthropology on the other. Not only is the irreversible cessation of whole-brain functioning an acceptable means of establishing human death, it "constitutes a human being's death from a Thomistic standpoint and can be understood as *the* event which indicates a rational soul's separation from the body it informs."[154]

The precise mechanism of death has important implications for the increasingly common practice of extracting organs from donors shortly after cardiac arrest. Indeed, the widespread acceptance of the neurological criteria has somewhat paradoxically

---

152. Smith, "Personhood and the Persistent Vegetative State," 56.

153. Ibid.

154. Eberl, "Thomistic Understanding of Human Death," 45, original emphasis.

heightened rather than lowered the requirements for what constitutes death. Under current US law, there are two recognized criteria for determining death, which can only be a single occurrence. Outside the ICU, this is not problematic. However, it is difficult to refute the widely accepted proposition that in actuality "there is no death of a human being without death of the brain."[155] Therefore, as William Sweet pointed out in 1978, the "time-honored criteria of stoppage of the heartbeat and circulation are indicative of death only when they persist long enough for the brain to die."[156]

There remains no documented case of recovery in situations where the criteria of brain death have been unequivocally met. This stands in contrast to numerous well-documented cases of recovery after cardiac death. Specifically, some patients have been declared dead after efforts to resuscitate them following cardiac arrest had failed, but nevertheless, they subsequently regained spontaneous circulation.[157] Ironically, there now is a lack of consensus on when death can be declared by the traditional means: "When the cardiologist pronounces

---

155. Werner Hacke, "Brain Death: An Artifact Created by Critical Care Medicine or—The Death of the Brain Has Always Been the Death of the Individuum," in *Signs of Death*, 87.

156. William Sweet, "Brain Death," *New England Journal of Medicine* 299.8 (August 24, 1978): 410, doi: 10.1056 /NEJM197808242990807.

157. Jerome Posner, "Alleged Awakenings from Prolonged Coma and Brain Death and Delivery of Live Babies from Brain-Dead Mothers Do Not Negate Brain Death," in *Signs of Death*, 116–122.

death as a result of cardiac standstill," the Pontifical Academy of Sciences carefully notes, "the diagnosis is less certain than in the circumstance of brain death."[158]

The Church has not specifically weighed in on death determination based on cardiac or circulatory function in the context of organ transplantation. Naturally, however, the overall approach in considering the matter would be the same as it has been for evaluating brain death. The Church does not make technical decisions but, with a sound anthropology always in mind, listens carefully to precisely what the medical community is saying. Following these same principles of methodological evaluation, concerns do arise, to which we finally now turn.

---

158. Battro et al., "Why the Concept of Brain Death Is Valid as a Definition of Death," XXVIII. "Many documented cases exist of patients pronounced dead after failure of cardiac resuscitation who have subsequently been discovered to be alive. It should be further stated that the traditional definition of natural loss of heart activity as 'death' is not satisfactory because it is now possible to keep the heart beating by artificial means, and blood circulation to the brain can be maintained artificially to a brain that is dead. Confusion arises from the presence of mechanical systems that artificially replace the role of the brain as the generator of the functioning of essential organs. Therefore, brain death is a much more certain diagnosis than heart death." See also, Johannes Bonelli, "Der status des hirntoten," *Imago Hominis* 20.2 (February 2013): 79–91; and David C. Magnus, Benjamin S. Wilfond, and Arthur L. Caplan, "Accepting Brain Death," *New England Journal of Medicine* 370.10 (March 6, 2014): 891–894, doi: 10.1056/NEJMp1400930.

6

Brain Death and the "Traditional" Understanding of Death

While the majority of organ donors today meet the neurological criteria for death, an increasing proportion of organ donation occurs among patients who are not brain-dead but who are said to meet the circulatory criteria for death. In essence, this refers to the traditional means of establishing death.

Before brain death was formally recognized, organ transplantation proceeded after breathing and heartbeat ceased and death was declared. Once the neurological criteria were accepted, however, donors almost exclusively were patients who had been declared brain dead. They were the ideal donors because their circulation could be maintained, keeping their organs perfused with oxygenated blood. The practice of procuring organs from non-brain-dead donors virtually ceased.

Few people die from brain death in the intensive care unit (ICU), however, which means that there are relatively few potential organ donors compared with the many people who could likely benefit from organ transplantation. For that reason, donation protocols based on the cessation of circulation were reintroduced about two decades ago. This initially was called non-heart-beating donation (NHBD) but eventually was changed to donation after cardiac death (DCD). The terminology was updated once again to donation after circulatory determination of death (DCDD) to reflect the fact that the loss of circulation rather than heart function per se is decisive.

But even this method of determining death is not so simple; in fact, it has proven, paradoxically, to be more controversial than brain death, particularly since medical authorities acknowledge that some DCDD donors may not actually be dead.

DCDD protocols have been steadily gathering momentum and constitute an increasing share of all organ transplants; between 2000 and 2008, DCDD donations increased almost seven-fold in the United States, accounting for 9.1 percent of all deceased donation in 2008.[1] In England, a greater percentage of organs are donated through DCDD protocols than through brain death protocols.[2] As of 2013 in the United King-

---

1. J. Y. Rhee et al., "The Impact of Variation in Donation after Cardiac Death Policies among Donor Hospitals: A Regional Analysis," *American Journal of Transplantation* 11.8 (August 2011): 1719, doi: 10.1111/j.1600 -6143.2011.03634.x.

2. James L. Bernat, "On Noncongruence between the Concept and Determination of Death," *Hastings Center Report* 43.6 (November–December 2013): 29, doi: 10.1002/hast.231.

dom, approximately one-third of all transplanted organs are procured through DCDD protocols.[3]

In what some regard as a heavy-handed federal mandate, DCDD protocols have become required in US hospitals since 2007. The specific objective of the mandate was to increase deceased donation by as much as 75 percent.[4] Hospitals must have a DCDD protocol in place if they wish to secure Medicare funding.[5] It is instructive to note, however, that in 2006 only about half of organ procurement organizations allowed that method of organ procurement.[6] Requiring institutions to include particular types of organ donation protocols seems to conflict with the voluntary spirit that is supposed to characterize the entire enterprise.

In short, DCDD protocols are currently a regular feature of the mainstream organ transplantation landscape. From the outset, however, their reemergence was

---

3. Ayyaz Ali et al., "Ethicality of Heart Transplantation from Donation after Circulatory Death Donors," *Journal of Clinical and Experimental Cardiology* suppl 9 (2013), 6, doi: 10.4172/2155-9880.S9-006.

4. Christopher Kaczor, "Philosophy and Theology," column, *National Catholic Bioethics Quarterly* 9.4 (Winter 2009): 776.

5. Sohaila Bastami et al., "Systematic Review of Attitudes toward Donation after Cardiac Death among Healthcare Providers and the General Public," *Critical Care Medicine* 41.3 (March 2013): 904, doi: 10.1097/CCM.0b013e31827585fe.

6. James L. Bernat, "Are Organ Donors after Cardiac Death Really Dead?," *Journal of Clinical Ethics* 17.2 (Summer 2006): 122.

met with strong objections and "widespread discomfort within the medical establishment."[7] There are a number of distinct criticisms of these types of protocols, notably concerns about conflicts of interest when managing potential donors and about the administration of certain pharmacological agents before death for the sake not of the donor but of the recipient.[8] The most prominent controversy, however, pertains to the lack of confidence in the determination of death itself, in particular the duration of circulatory arrest needed to have moral certainty that the asystolic patient has died.

Review of the Procedure

Typically, a potential DCDD donor has sustained severe neurological injury but is not brain-dead. Given the severity of the prognosis, some families may elect to withhold further treatment and allow the loved one to die. In this context, death is expected to occur rapidly,

---

7. Peter A. Clark and Uday Deshmukh, "Non-heart-beating Organ Donation and Catholic Ethics," *National Catholic Bioethics Quarterly* 4.3 (Autumn 2004): 540.

8. For a comprehensive review of the various objections to DCDD protocols, see Ari R. Joffe et al., "Donation after Cardiocirculatory Death: A Call for a Moratorium Pending Full Public Disclosure and Fully Informed Consent," *Philosophy, Ethics, and Humanities in Medicine* 6 (2011): 17, doi: 10.1186/1747-5341-6-17. For a review that reaches a more favorable conclusion about the permissibility of DCDD protocols under specific conditions, see James M. Dubois, "Organ Transplantation: An Ethical Road Map," *National Catholic Bioethics Quarterly* 2.3 (Autumn 2002): 413–453.

since the patient is too compromised to maintain cardio-pulmonary function for long without assistance. Once this decision has been made independently, the issue of organ donation may be broached.

If consent is granted, then the withdrawal of care can be coordinated to facilitate organ removal by a separate surgical team shortly after death occurs. Timing here is of the essence. If too much time elapses after circulation ceases, then the viability of organs may be compromised. If too little time elapses after circulation stops, death may not yet have occurred.

Not every person who consents to this method of donation actually becomes a donor. If the patient does not die within a relatively short period after life support is withdrawn, then the procedure is called off and the patient is returned to palliative care. Typically, this window is not more than one hour, but this varies considerably. Some hospitals permit an interval of up to three hours, while some do not specify one at all.[9] According to one study, at least 20 percent of patients in DCDD protocols do not die fast enough after the ventilator is withdrawn to actually become donors.[10]

Historical Context for the Primacy of the Brain

Assuming that cardiac arrest occurs soon after treatment is withdrawn, there is a period of observation after

---

9.   Rhee et al., Variation in Donation," 1721–1722.

10. Nancy Valko, "Organ Donation: Crossing the Line," *MercatorNet*, October 6, 2011, https://www.mercatornet.com/.

the cessation of circulation to ensure that it is irreversible. No one would declare death the moment the heart stops, because circulatory function could restart on its own or be restarted by technical intervention. The question becomes, how long must one wait?

There are a number of different answers to that question. Most institutions in the United States have precariously settled on a waiting period of two to five minutes. The first thing to recall, however, is that the determination of death in DCDD settings is *prospective* by nature. The very act of waiting for something implies it has not yet arrived. Immediately after the onset of asystole, no one contests the possibility that death may not have occurred yet.

By contrast, brain death determinations are *retrospective*. Clinical tests conducted well after the moment of death confirm that it has already occurred. Death is a single, unitary event, and current medical knowledge strongly suggests that we may properly take a neurocentric view of death. For instance, a person can overcome the loss of cardiac or pulmonary function. But medical technology simply cannot compensate for the complete loss of critical brain functions in the same way. It can replace all the vital organs—heart, lungs, kidneys, livers, and such—with the exception of the brain.

In their 1982 book *Philosophy in Medicine*, Charles Culver and Bernard Gert put that observation in the following terms:

> Because of current ventilation/circulation technology, permanent loss of spontaneous cardiopulmonary functioning is no longer necessarily predictive of permanent nonfunctioning of the organism as a whole.

176

> Consider a conscious, talking patient who is unable to breathe because of suffering from poliomyelitis and who requires an iron lung (thus having permanent loss of spontaneous pulmonary function), who has developed asystole (loss of spontaneous heartbeat) requiring a permanent pacemaker (thus having permanent loss of spontaneous cardiac function). It would be absurd to regard such a person as dead. ... The heart and lungs now seem to have no unique relationship to the functioning of the organism as a whole. Continued artificially supported cardiopulmonary function is no longer perfectly correlated with life, and permanent loss of spontaneous cardiopulmonary functioning is no longer perfectly correlated with death.[11]

In other words, the loss of cardiopulmonary function is not a sufficient cause for death. The irreversible loss of critical brain function, on the other hand, is both a necessary and sufficient condition for death. As a result of technological advances, the primacy of the brain has become recognized in a manner that was not previously demonstrable. We now know that death—traditionally recognized by the cessation of heartbeat and circulation—cannot be reliably confirmed until the brain has been destroyed.[12]

---

11. Charles M. Culver and Bernard Gert, *Philosophy in Medicine: Conceptual and Ethical Issues in Medicine and Psychiatry* (Oxford, UK: Oxford University Press, 1982), 186.

12. William H. Sweet, "Brain Death," *New England Journal of Medicine* 299.8 (August 24, 1978): 410.

Several countries officially recognize the primacy of the brain in that regard—that all death is ultimately brain death. For example, in the context of organ transplantation, Switzerland explicitly links the two means of determining death, tying the cardiopulmonary standard to the irreversible loss of brain function: "Death can either occur through the 'irreversible cessation of the functions of the brain, including the brainstem, as a result of primary brain damage or disorder; [or through] permanent cardiac arrest, which reduces or abolishes the cerebral circulation, until the irreversible cessation of the functions of the brain and brainstem—and thus death—ensues (death after cardiac arrest).'"[13]

The United States, however, ultimately decided on a formulation that refers to both cardiopulmonary and neurologic functions without specifying the relationship between them. The Uniform Determination of Death Act (UDDA) stipulates that "an individual who has sustained either (1) irreversible cessation of circulatory and respiratory functions, or (2) irreversible cessation of all functions of the entire brain, including the brainstem, is dead. A determination of death must be made in accordance with accepted medical standards."[14]

---

13. Swiss Academy of Medical Sciences, *The Determination of Death in the Context of Organ Transplantation: Medical-Ethical Guidelines* (Bern, Switzerland: SAMS, 2011), 5, quoted in Settimio Monteverde and Annette Rid, "Controversies on the Determination of Death: Perspectives from Switzerland," *Swiss Medical Weekly* 142 (August 17, 2012): w13667, doi: 10.4414/smw.2012.13667.

14. *Uniform Determination of Death Act*, National Conference of Commissioners on Uniform State Laws, 1980, §1.

It is not difficult to appreciate a desire to maintain continuity with the traditional standard for recognizing death, but this formulation is not without prominent detractors. They argue that a neurocentric understanding of death is most appropriate because what is needed is a single, coherent standard, rather than a means or test by which to determine that a given standard has been met.

In 1982, James Bernat, Charles Culver, and Bernard Gert argued that the statute recommended in 1981 by the President's Commission for the study of Ethical Problems in Medicine and Biomedical and Behavioral Research—which made its way into the UDDA—should not be adopted. Not only is it too ambiguous, but "it elevates the irreversible cessation of cardiopulmonary functioning to the level of a standard of death, when it is really only a test, although a test that may be used in most circumstances. Permanent cessation of spontaneous cardiopulmonary functioning works as a test of death only in the absence of artificial cardiopulmonary support because only there does it produce the true standard of death—the irreversible cessation of all brain functions."[15]

Despite the fact that laypeople might understandably look to the loss of cardiopulmonary functioning as an indication that death has occurred, the authors contend that the law should correspond to our physiological understanding of the mechanism of death. The fact of the matter, they maintain, is that

> informed medical opinion is now virtually unanimous that a person is dead when and only when the entire

15. James L. Bernat, Charles M. Culver, and Bernard Gert, "Defining Death in Theory and Practice," *Hastings Center Report* 12.1 (February 1982): 8, doi: 10.2307/3560613.

brain, including the brainstem, has permanently ceased to function. … A conceptually satisfactory statute would not need to mention cessation of cardiopulmonary function at all. It would be sufficient to include only irreversible cessation of whole brain functioning and allow physicians to select validated and agreed-upon tests (prolonged absence of spontaneous cardiopulmonary function would be one) to measure irreversible cessation of whole brain function.[16]

A standard must capture both the necessary and sufficient condition for death. We must be able to say, as they put it, "If the standard is fulfilled, the person is dead; if it is not fulfilled, the person is not dead. Irreversible cessation of all brain functions is such a standard. If it has occurred, the person is dead; if it has not occurred, the person is not dead, no matter what has happened to the heart, lungs, or any other organ."[17]

With these important considerations in mind, they ultimately deem the current working definition of death "seriously misleading" because it essentially presents two standards of death without properly reconciling them. To correctly distinguish between a standard of and test for death, and between spontaneous and artificially mediated functions, they would have preferred the statute to read as follows:

An individual who has sustained irreversible cessation of all functions of the entire brain, including the brainstem, is dead. (a) In the absence of artificial means of cardiopulmonary support, death (the irreversible cessation of all brain functions) may be determined

16. Ibid., 6, 8.

17. Ibid., 8.

by the prolonged absence of spontaneous circulatory and respiratory functions. (b) In the presence of artificial means of cardiopulmonary support, death (the irreversible cessation of all brain functions) must be determined by tests of brain function. In both situations, the determination of death must be made in accordance with accepted medical standards.[18]

The advantage of this formulation is its accuracy and clarity. There is a single standard that best corresponds to the single phenomenon of death, yet it allows for death to be declared by the traditional cardiopulmonary criteria in the vast majority of cases. These cases, by and large, do not involve the ICU or organ transplantation. These considerations remain as valid as ever. Nevertheless, the mainstream justification for DCDD protocols today amounts to an attempt to wiggle away from the critical consideration, as concisely articulated above, that the true standard of death is the irreversible cessation of brain function.

Single Operational Definition

This kind of deflection is similarly evident in more recent attempts to rectify untenable discrepancies in defining death. In 2014, leading international practitioners released a "single operational definition" for death: "The permanent loss of capacity for consciousness and all brainstem functions, as a consequence of permanent cessation of circulation or catastrophic brain injury."[19]

---

18. Ibid.

19. Sam D. Shemie et al., "International Guideline Development for the Determination of Death," *Intensive Care Medicine* 40.6 (June 2014): 788, doi: 10.1007/s00134 -014-3242-7.

There are several things to note about this definition. First, it is clearly neurocentric, requiring the death of the brain regardless of how (or where in the body) any fatal breakdown originates and progresses. Second, it specifies the loss of "all brainstem functions" in addition to consciousness, which is significant because previous formulations proposed by some of the same authors boiled it down to "capacity to breathe."[20] This is essentially a whole–brain–death standard. Third, by selecting permanence in lieu of irreversibility, they have opted for a less rigorous standard for the sake of accessing viable organs sooner. By abandoning the gold standard of irreversibility, they make peace with ambiguity because death cannot be ascertained with sufficient certainty by any lesser standard.

In 2017, Bernat, who helped develop the single operational definition of death, coauthored another iteration of this overall approach: "Death could thus be defined as the permanent cessation of brain functions, determined either by the permanent cessation of brain circulation in cases of circulatory cessation (including to the brain) or by the irreversible cessation of brain functions in cases of severe brain injury."[21] This elucidates the distinction between permanence and irreversibility that is professed to be decisive in the context of cardiac-based organ

20. D. Gardiner et al., "International Perspective on the Diagnosis of Death," *British Journal of Anaesthesia* 108 suppl 1 (January 2012): i14–i28, doi: 10.1093/bja/aer397.

21. Anne L. Dalle Ave and James L. Bernat, "Donation after Brain Circulation Determination of Death," *BMC Medical Ethics* 18.1 (February 23, 2017): 19, doi: 10.1186/s12910-017-0173-1.

donation protocols. It does offer welcome precision by stressing that circulation to the brain rather than cardiac function is conclusive, although their introduction of a new term—donation after brain circulation determination of death (DBCDD)—might be slightly disorienting.

Nevertheless, the overriding point remains: these authors steadfastly uphold that brain function should be *the* determinative characteristic of death, yet they shrink from that very conclusion by proposing two different thresholds for an event that by definition can have only one.

Two Possibilities

Once the heartbeat stops and circulation begins to cease, there are only two ways that death can be forestalled: the patient spontaneously recovers vital functions on his own, which is known as autoresuscitation, or other individuals act to restore vital functions by technical means such as cardiopulmonary resuscitation (CPR).

Autoresuscitation is not a well-studied phenomenon, and the rather little knowledge we possess comes mainly from limited observational studies.[22] One 2010 review concluded that there is not enough evidence to justify or invalidate the recommended waiting period between the onset of cardiac arrest and a death determination. This points to the need for prospective studies to increase our knowledge about this particular matter, especially since

---

22. Jill Sweney and Susan Bratton, "Acceptance of Circulatory Determination of Death and Donation: What Types, Limits, and Safeguards?," *Critical Care Medicine* 41.3 (March 2013): 934, doi: 10.1097/CCM.0b013e31827c0104.

clinicians remain concerned about it. When that review was updated in 2018, it found several documented cases of autoresuscitation in both adult and pediatric populations, which occurred as late as ten minutes following the cessation of CPR and three minutes following the withdrawal of life support. They concluded that while further clarification about this phenomenon is still needed, autoresuscitation is clearly a matter that clinicians must account for before declaring death.[23]

In one study, which reviewed seventy-three DCDD cases between 2000 and 2008 at the University of Maryland Medical Center, no donors autoresuscitated after the two-minute mark. The authors concluded that a two-minute waiting period is sufficient for determining death in the DCDD context. This is but one observational study, although it does seem to correspond to the broader evidence base. The authors acknowledged the lack of consensus on a minimum waiting period and the variability in clinical practice.[24]

Indeed, some critics maintain that the actual threshold has yet to be ascertained, because the two-to five-minute waiting period originally was based on data from only twelve patients. A study would have to document zero cases of autoresuscitation in a sample

23. Laura Hornby, Sonny Dhanani, and Sam D. Shemie, "Update of a Systematic Review of Autoresuscitation after Cardiac Arrest," *Critical Care Medicine* 46.3 (March 2018): e271, doi: 10.1097/CCM.0000000000002920.

24. Kevin N. Sheth et al., "Autoresuscitation after Asystole in Patients Being Considered for Organ Donation," *Critical Care Medicine* 40.1 (January 2012): 158–161, doi: 10.1097/CCM.0b013e31822f0b2a.

of 10,516 patients to rule out an incidence of one per one thousand.[25]

Even if the precise point in time at which autoresuscitation may be ruled out were known with great confidence, however, we would still need to consider the possibility that a person could be resuscitated by external means even if it would not be attempted.

Successful resuscitation has occurred after prolonged periods of cardiac arrest, challenging the assertion that the loss of brain function is irreversible after ten minutes of asystole. For instance, 10 to 15 percent of patients who are resuscitated more than five to six minutes (up to thirty-five minutes) after cardiac arrest recover normal or only moderately impaired brain function.[26]

The common understanding of death corresponds to the common understanding of irreversibility. This intuitive and widely accepted notion must be maintained, and other considerations must not be allowed to supersede this threshold.

No one contests the fact that in DCDD, it would be unethical to attempt CPR on the patient after the decision to withdraw life support. Some maintain, however, that patients may be considered dead once autoresuscitation is deemed impossible, because it would be ethically

---

25. Scott D. Halpern and Robert D. Truog, "Organ Donors after Circulatory Determination of Death: Not Necessarily Dead, and It Does Not Necessarily Matter," *Critical Care Medicine* 38.3 (March 2010): 1011, doi: 10.1097 /CCM.0b013e3181cc1228.

26. Monteverde and Rid, "Controversies on the Determination of Death."

and legally impermissible to attempt to reverse the patient's condition.[27] But this is not convincing, because it conflates what would be unethical with *what is*. We are concerned with establishing the underlying reality: whether a person has actually died, not whether it would be wrong to try to revive him.

Varying Waiting Periods

Relatively little is known about brain activity following cardiopulmonary arrest; the point at which irreversible damage occurs has not been definitively established. Several authorities have settled on a threshold of ten minutes. In 1981, the President's Commission noted that brain tissue in adults with normal body temperature cannot survive more than ten minutes with a complete lack of circulation.[28]

According to the textbook *Core Topics in Neuroanaesthesia and Neurointensive Care*, it is possible to fully

---

27. James DuBois's position is effectively countered in Christopher Kaczor, "Organ Donation following Cardiac Death: Conflicts of Interest, Ante Mortem Interventions, and Determinations of Death," in *The Ethics of Organ Transplantation*, ed. Steven Jensen (Washington, DC: Catholic University of America Press, 2011), 95–113. See also Jason T. Eberl, *Thomistic Principles and Bioethics* (London: Routledge, 2006), 124–125.

28. President's Commission for the Study of Ethical Problems in Medicine and Biomedical and Behavioral Research, *Defining Death: A Report on the Medical, Legal and Ethical Issues in the Determination of Death* (Washington, DC: Government Printing Office, 1981), 164.

recover brain function within eleven minutes of asystole. After this, circulatory arrest probably is irreversible.[29]

Other research contests that even ten minutes is sufficient to establish irreversibility, and a 2011 study by an international team of practitioners concluded that brain function can likely be recovered more than fifteen minutes after circulation ceases.[30] Still others, such as Alan Shewmon, who subscribe to a circulatory criterion of death have posited that twenty to thirty minutes following loss of circulation is typically required to establish irreversibility.[31]

As with brain death guidelines, there is significant variability between DCDD protocols within countries and internationally. Protocols don't always clearly convey that the waiting period is to commence at the point of observed loss of circulation and end with the declaration of death; approximately one-third of US protocols reflect a "fundamental misunderstanding" in this regard.[32]

---

29. Gina M. Sanchez, "Objections to Donation after Cardiac Death: A Violation of Human Dignity," *National Catholic Bioethics Quarterly* 12.1 (Spring 2012): 60, citing Basil Matta, David K. Menon, and Martin Smith, *Core Topics in Neuroanaesthesia and Neurointensive Care* (Cambridge, UK: Cambridge University Press, 2011), 472.

30. Joffe et al., "Donation after Cardiocirculatory Death."

31. Kaczor, "Philosophy and Theology," 780.

32. Jennifer E. Fugate et al., "Variability in Donation after Cardiac Death Protocols: A National Survey," *Transplantation* 91.4 (February 27, 2011): 389, doi: 10.1097/TP.0b013e318204ee96.

Several different time intervals exist in the United States, and according to a 2011 survey, 16 percent of protocols provided no specifications whatsoever.[33] Typically, two to five minutes are required. The Institute of Medicine recommends five minutes at minimum. The Society of Critical Care Medicine and the National Conference on Organ Donation recommend no less than two and no more than five minutes. In one institutional protocol in Denver, the specified waiting time is as short as seventy-five seconds. This protocol proved extremely controversial, particularly since soon after it was adopted, the hearts of three infants were extracted for transplantation seventy-five seconds after asystole.

There also is considerable variability internationally, and the required waiting period can be as long as twenty minutes. It is noteworthy that only the Unites States, Australia, and New Zealand permit waiting periods as short as two minutes.[34] Italy has settled on an interval of twenty minutes; the Italian National Bioethics Committee explicitly argues that a two- to five-minute interval is too short to ensure irreversible loss of encephalic functions. It maintains that such a short interval

---

33. Ibid., 387. This study also found that 44 percent of the protocols failed to specify the methods by which cardiac death was to be determined, and 25 percent did not explicitly specify that there should be a strict separation between the transplant team and the clinicians involved in the discontinuation of care and the declaration of death.

34. Sonny Dhanani et al., "Variability in the Determination of Death after Cardiac Arrest: A Review of Guidelines and Statements," *Journal of Intensive Care Medicine* 27.4 (July–August 2012): 240, doi: 10.1177/0885066610396993..

risks transforming the dead donor rule into the "dying donor rule."[35]

Sweden also uses twenty minutes as the mark.[36] In fact, Sweden takes an officially neurocentric view of death. This, in turn, has implications for how physicians determine death precipitated by cardio-respiratory failure. Since brain death is their sole standard, they presume it has occurred once the absence of heartbeat and respiration have been observed for twenty minutes. At this point, death can be pronounced, but a neurological examination or angiography is conducted on potential organ donors.[37] Leading institutions in countries such as Holland and Switzerland have settled on ten minutes. The Maastricht protocol also specifies ten minutes.[38]

---

35. Italian National Bioethics, "Committee, Criteria for Ascertaining Death," opinion (June 24, 2010), http://bioetica.governo.it/. See also Ornella Piazza et al., "Maximum Tolerable Warm Ischaemia Time in Transplantation from Non-heart-beating-donors," *Trends in Anaesthesia and Critical Care* 3.2 (April 2013): 72–76, doi: 10.1016/j.tacc.2013.01.002.

36. Ari R. Joffe, "The Ethics of Donation and Transplantation: Are Definitions of Death Being Distorted for Organ Transplantation?," *Philosophy, Ethics and Humanities in Medicine* 2 (2007): 28, doi: 10.1186/1747-5341-2-28.

37. Alister Browne, "The Ethics of Organ Donation after Cardiocirculatory Death: Do the Guidelines of the Canadian Council for Donation and Transplantation Measure Up?," *Open Medicine* 4.2 (2010): E131.

38. Italian National Bioethics Committee, "Criteria for Ascertaining Death," 24.

The existence of widely varying waiting periods suggests that a person could be declared dead prematurely in one region but not another. It seems likely that the prospect of organ donation is largely responsible for this variability. At a minimum, it exerts pressure to trim that time frame as much as possible. Doing so is not necessarily wrong per se. After all, the ethics of all vital-organ transplantation hinges on whether a person is alive or dead. Once a patient is dead, it is permissible to do what had previously been forbidden. Nonetheless, the necessary haste may strike many as unseemly, and reasonably so.

In fact, an international team of scholars concluded in 2013 that medical professionals and the public hold "deep-rooted concerns" about DCDD protocols. Concerns were not limited to a single issue, but included potential conflicts of interest, the use of premortem interventions without the explicit consent of the donor, and the lack of standardization; a "recurring theme," however, was concern over violating the dead donor rule.[39]

Here we begin to see the difficulty of satisfying the most important requirement: moral certainty. There is, at present, no consensus on the duration of circulatory arrest required to establish its irreversibility. In DCDD scenarios, we know with moral certainty that a patient is dying. We lack, however, the moral certainty to say at a given point in time, such as two minutes or even five minutes after the onset of asystole, that the patient has died.

---

39. Bastami et al., "Systematic Review of Attitudes toward Donation," 897, 902, 903.

In fact, it is widely acknowledged that in DCDD, death has not been established after five minutes of asystole but "will occur many minutes later, when the brain has become totally infarcted as a result of anoxic damage."[40] The authors of a thorough review in *Critical Care Medicine* expressed that commonly held concern in their conclusion: "With neither cardiac nor neurologic function being irretrievably lost until after many minutes of asystole, it seems that many, if not all cases of DCD, may involve organ donation from patients who are not yet biologically dead."[41]

It is for this reason that qualms about DCDD protocols are well grounded. In fact, those who currently defend them tend not base their justifications on the grounds that the donor is unequivocally dead because irreversibility has been established, but on other reasons, as we shall see.

Retroactive Negation?

As a means of framing this most pertinent issue—the point in time when we may properly deem a patient dead because of the cessation of circulation—it will be helpful to describe the evolution of the position taken by Bernat,

---

40. Steven Laureys, "Death, Unconsciousness and the Brain," *Nature Reviews Neuroscience* 6.11 (November 2005): 902, doi: 10.1038/nrn1789.

41. Michael Souter and Gail Van Norman, "Ethical Controversies at End of Life after Traumatic Brain Injury: Defining Death and Organ Donation," *Critical Care Medicine* 38.9 suppl (September 2010): S508, doi: 10.1097 /CCM.0b013e3181ec5354.

one of the most steady and influential voices over the last several decades with respect to death determination. He serves as an instructive point of reference because he is an authoritative voice and a well-regarded, steadfast defender of the dead donor rule.

When he wrote "A Defense of the Whole-Brain Concept of Death" in 1998, he argued convincingly that the definitive criterion or standard for death pertains to the loss of "clinical functions of the entire brain" because this is "the only condition that is both necessary and sufficient for death."[42] This is consistent with the explicitly neurocentric position he and his colleagues coherently championed in the 1980s.

The cardiorespiratory criteria are sufficient, provided irreversibility is established, but they are not necessary. As a result, Bernat identified a serious problem with DCDD protocols, in particular one at a Pittsburgh hospital which required only a two-minute waiting period:

> It is not clear that the patients are dead within the first few minutes of apnea and asystole. It takes considerably longer than a few minutes for the brain and other organs to be destroyed from cessation of circulation and lack of oxygen. Moreover, it takes longer than this time for the cessation of heartbeat and breathing to be unequivocally irreversible, a prerequisite for death. As proof of this assertion, if cardiopulmonary resuscitation were performed within a few minutes of cardiorespiratory arrest, it is likely that some of the purportedly '"dead" patients could be successfully

---

42. James L. Bernat, "A Defense of the Whole-Brain Concept of Death," *Hastings Center Report* 28.2 (March–April 1998): 19.

resuscitated to spontaneous heartbeat and some intact brain function. Unfortunately for the goals of organ procurement, the elapsed time that would be necessary to assure certainty of irreversibility of apnea and asystole also constitutes the time during which the potentially transplantable organs would be destroyed, rendering them unsuitable for transplantation.[43]

Here we see with abundant clarity one of the chief ironies surrounding the determination of death and organ transplantation. Some opponents of the brain death standard prefer a circulatory standard, supposing that this is a surer means of determining death. But this method turns out to provide less certainty than the neurological criteria.

It is perfectly ethical to forgo resuscitation attempts, since the original, legitimate decision to withdraw life support should be respected. However, this imperative implies that the person may still be alive;[44] acknowledging all this, Bernat plainly concludes that "at the time the organs are being procured in the Pittsburgh protocol, death has not yet occurred."[45]

Other potential features of the process reinforce that conclusion. For example, there is the practice of using extracorporeal membrane oxygenation (ECMO) as an organ preservation technique after a declaration of

43. Ibid., 20. He also writes, "The cessation of heartbeat and breathing must be prolonged because their absence must be of sufficient duration for the brain to become diffusely infarcted and for the cessation of heartbeat and breathing conclusively to be irreversible."

44. Joffe et al., "Donation after Cardiocirculatory Death."

45. Bernat, "A Defense of the Whole-Brain Concept," 20.

death but prior to organ extraction. The basic purpose of ECMO in this setting is to restore a measure of circulation to keep the desired organs perfused with oxygenated blood. One 2005 study estimated that ECMO could increase the donor pool by 33 percent.[46] Bernat, along with many others, has objected to this practice on numerous occasions. He writes that ECMO should be discouraged on the grounds that "by re-establishing blood flow to the brain, [it] *retroactively negates* the prior death determination."[47]

The irreversible nature of death itself plainly entails that it cannot be "retroactively negated." Such a locution raises red flags. Elsewhere, Bernat explains his disapproval of ECMO by drawing on a coherent physiological understanding about the mechanism of death: The practice "retroactively negates the physiologic justification for declaring the DCDD donor dead. By allowing reperfusion of the brain and thereby preventing brain destruction, it interrupts the otherwise inevitable progression from permanent loss of circulation and respiration to

---

46. Sanchez, "Objections to Donation after Cardiac Death," 60, citing Joseph F. Magliocca et al., "Extracorporeal Support for Organ Donation after Cardiac Death Effectively Expands the Donor Pool," *Journal of Trauma* 58.6 (June 2005): 1095–1101.

47. James L. Bernat, "Controversies in Defining and Determining Death in Critical Care," *Nature Reviews Neurology* 9.3 (March 2013): 170, doi: 10.1038/nrneurol.2013.12, emphasis added. See also, James L. Bernat et al., "The Circulatory-Respiratory Determination of Death in Organ Donation," *Critical Care Medicine* 38.3 (March 2010): 963–970, doi: 10.1097/CCM.0b013e3181c58916.

irreversible loss. Restoring brain circulation also raises the possibility of retaining donor consciousness and the consequent potential for suffering."[48]

ECMO serves as a reminder that in the context of organ transplantation, treating permanence and irreversibility as roughly equivalent is problematic because it does not correspond to the actual living or dead state of the patient with sufficient precision. The fact that a procedure has the potential to "retroactively negate" a death determination can only mean that the patient may still be alive at that point in time. This stands in contrast with the fact that no intervention has even the remote possibility of retroactively negating a death determination made by the neurological criteria.

There is also an invasive, modified form of ECMO known as extracorporeal interval support for organ retrieval (EISOR), which explicitly seeks to prevent oxygenated blood from reaching the heart and brain after circulation has been reestablished. The only reason to do this is to ensure full brain destruction when there is a possibility that it has not occurred. A conclusion thus forces itself on the observer: if that is the case and, as ECMO itself demonstrates, circulatory arrest is not yet irreversible, then the donor is not yet dead.[49] The fact that ECMO or other aggressive techniques such as

48. Bernat et al., "The Circulatory-Respiratory Determination of Death," 967.

49. Steve Mikochik, "The Church, ECMO, and DCD Organ Recovery" (presentation, Fourth International Congress on ECMO [Extracorporeal Membrane Oxygenation] Therapy, Dauphin, Pennsylvania, October 19, 2013).

cardiopulmonary bypass have the potential to revive the donor is the very reason that expert panels in both the United States and the United Kingdom reject the application of such technologies in these settings.[50]

In philosophical terms, the reanimation of circulation and the revival of the brain before it has been destroyed could reasonably be construed as evidence that the active potentialities of the soul are still present. The body at that point in time is still disposed to support the soul. Likewise, any person in a state of circulatory arrest but who receives CPR in the nick of time and survives always retained sufficient physiological foundation to support the soul.

Interpretation Not Facts

These factors are openly acknowledged by those with differing ethical outlooks. It is in the realm of ethical interpretation that opinions diverge. Bernat has never withdrawn his contention that individuals involved in DCDD may still be alive, but he now favors current DCDD protocols. He has not changed his view on the mechanism by which death occurs or on the primacy of brain death. New facts have not led to a secure conclusion that death always occurs five minutes following asystole and apnea.

His present view amounts, as he honestly acknowledges, to an ethical interpretation of these known facts. All things considered, he now feels an exception to the dead donor rule—the fundamental axiom he has long

---

50. Sweney and Bratton, "Acceptance of Circulatory Determination of Death and Donation," 934.

upheld—should be permissible in the case of current DCDD protocols. He concludes this 2006 essay with a personal observation regarding the evolution of his perspective:

> For example, in the current practice of organ donation after cardiac death (formerly known as non-heart-beating organ donation), I and others raised the question of whether the organ donor patients were truly dead after only five minutes of asystole. The five-minute rule was accepted by the Institute of Medicine as the point at which death could be declared and the organs procured. Ours was a biologically valid criticism because, at least in theory, some such patients could be resuscitated after five minutes of asystole and still retain measurable brain function. If that was true, they were not yet dead at that point so their death declaration was premature.
>
> But thereafter I changed my position to support programs of organ donation after cardiac death. I decided that it was justified to accept a compromise on this biological point when I realized that donor patients, if not already dead at five minutes of asystole, were incipiently and irreversibly dying because they could not auto-resuscitate and no one would attempt their resuscitation. Because their loss of circulatory and respiratory functions was permanent if not yet irreversible, there would be no difference whatsoever in their outcomes if their death were declared after five minutes of asystole or after 60 minutes of asystole. I concluded that, from a public policy perspective, accepting the permanent loss of circulatory and respiratory functions rather than requiring their irreversible loss was justified. The good accruing to the organ recipient, the donor patient, and the donor family resulting from organ donation justified

overlooking the biological shortcoming because, although the difference in the death criteria was real, it was inconsequential.[51]

It is easy to appreciate the clarity and honesty of Bernat's writing. His acceptance of a biological compromise, however, remains contentious.

Bernat has settled on the term *irreversible* as the standard pertaining to the loss of all clinically determined brain function, but *permanent* as the standard pertaining to the loss of circulatory and respiratory functions.[52] Resorting to two differentiated standards for determining death, however, does not square with the unitary phenomenon he otherwise convincingly champions. He acknowledges that this is an interpretive maneuver rather than a consistent, accurate reflection of the biological phenomenon of death.

In accordance with biology and ontology, the requirement of irreversibility is also enshrined in the law, which means that some organs are procured before

---

51. James L. Bernat, "The Whole-Brain Concept of Death Remains Optimum Public Policy," *Journal of Law, Medicine and Ethics* 34.1 (March 2006): 41, doi: 10.1111/j.1748 -720X.2006.00006.x.

52. See, for example, James L. Bernat, "Contemporary Controversies in the Definition of Death," in *Progress in Brain Research*, vol. 177, *Coma Science: Clinical and Ethical Implications*, ed. Steven Laureys, Nicholas D. Schiff, and Adrian M. Owen (Philadelphia: Elsevier, 2009), 22. "DCD protocols also have raised important medical and social questions over how soon physicians can declare death once circulation and respiration have ceased permanently but before they have ceased irreversibly."

donors are legally dead.[53] The clinical determination of whole-brain death, it may be said, does not always conform to the law, because some signs of brain activity might still be present. In those instances, medical authorities acknowledge the discrepancy with the law but nonetheless maintain that death is established by the clinical criteria.

Not all are comfortable with using permanence as a proxy for irreversibility. Some who feel that DCDD should proceed even if the donors are not yet dead claim that this equivalency is a "rhetorical device" or "semantic manipulation."[54] Others deem that DCDD relies on a "subtle fudging of the truth" which routinely amounts to a "*de facto* violation" of the dead donor rule.[55]

53. Jerry Menikoff, "The Importance of Being Dead: Non-heart-beating Organ Donation," *Issues in Law and Medicine* 18.1 (Summer 2002): 3. "An examination of the legal definition of death suggests that organs are indeed being procured from some of these people prior to their being legally dead. Moreover, the fact that the donors have consented to these procedures does not eliminate reason for concern regarding this state of affairs, since patient autonomy must at times be overridden in pursuance of important social goals."

54. Robert M. Sade, "Brain Death, Cardiac Death, and the Dead Donor Rule," *Journal of the South Carolina Medical Association* 107.4 (August 2011): 147–148.

55. Robert D. Truog and Franklin G. Miller, "Counterpoint: Are Donors after Circulatory Death Really Dead, and Does It Matter? No and Not Really," *Chest* 138.1 (July 2010):16, 18, doi: 10.1378/chest.10-0657. These authors are proponents of organ transplantation, even though they claim no donor today is actually dead. But what they

The key question pertaining to DCDD protocols, as posed by Bernat himself, takes the form of a concession: "Will society tolerate knowing that patients are serving as vital organ donors before they are unequivocally dead, once this fact is better publicized?" He provides his own answer:

> I conclude that our society will permit the practice for three reasons. First the claim of some critics that "DCD is killing an almost dead patient for organs" is simply false. As Menikoff explains, the organ donation does not cause or even accelerate the patient's death. DCD patients are dead when their brains are destroyed by cessation of breathing and circulation, as evolving inevitably over minutes from being permanently lost to irreversibly lost. If critics wished to assign causation to the death of the patient, what "killed" the DCD patient was the earlier withdrawal of life-sustaining therapy, an act that

---

write here is difficult to dismiss: "In particular, if one holds that the [dead donor rule] is an inviolate principle of organ donation, then the difference between 'dying' and 'dead' becomes crucial. Even a very slim chance of a false positive makes a difference. If the patient is, in fact, not dead or not known to be dead at the time of the declaration of death, then the [dead donor rule] has been violated. ... Although Bernat offers no reasons for accepting permanence as a valid stand-in for irreversibility other than a misplaced reference to accepted medical practice, we believe there are sound reasons for rejecting this equivalence. The difference between life and death is an ontologic distinction; it is about two different 'states of the world.' But under Bernat's formulation, this fundamental distinction becomes dependent on the intentions and actions of those surrounding the patient at the time of death" (17).

is widely practiced and constitutionally protected, and, according to DCD protocols, would have been performed irrespective of organ donation. Second, most DCD patients will not care if they are declared dead earlier in a process that quickly and inevitably achieves irreversibility, because they wish to donate, and the difference to them is utterly inconsequential. And third, in my experience, most physicians seem to express no problem declaring DCD patients dead at five minutes of asystole, because doing so is consistent with their current practice of using a permanence standard elsewhere in the hospital.[56]

The second and third reasons he cites—the wishes of the patients and the feelings of the doctors—cannot be determinative. The first of the reasons he flags, however, needs some clarification: should the dead donor rule—an ethical axiom that is not formally enshrined into law—be understood to mean that we may not actively kill the patient or hasten his or her death by extracting organs? Or does it primarily mean that donors simply must be dead before their vital organs may be removed? Both seem required according to the commonly accepted interpretation that "organ procurement should never kill a patient and may begin only after the donor has been declared dead."[57] Bernat, however, concludes that violating the dead donor rule "in this case does not lead to the death of the patient, so its *raison d'etre* does not apply in DCD."[58]

---

56. Bernat, "Are Organ Donors after Cardiac Death Really Dead?," 129.

57. Eberl, *Thomistic Principles and Bioethics*, 121.

58. Bernat, "Are Organ Donors after Cardiac Death Really Dead?," 129.

Organ extraction after DCDD may not constitute killing. However, this does not necessarily mean that avoiding direct killing is the sole purpose of the dead donor rule. Suppose that it may be conceded that organ procurement neither directly kills the patient nor hastens his death and that the patient or surrogate has expressed a decision to donate. If the patient is not dead at the moment procurement begins, the procedure still constitutes a compromise—however minor it may be—to the dead donor rule.

Why Two Standards?

Furthermore, the claim that these circumstances justify an exception to the dead donor rule cannot be reconciled with another commonly desired goal: greater standardization of the DCDD guidelines and a corresponding increase in uniformity of clinical practice.[59]

---

59. See, for example, ibid. "We need greater standardization of physicians' practices in determining death in DCD patients. It is well known that DCD protocols for determining death vary somewhat among organ procurement organizations, particularly in the durations of asystole necessary to determine death. Just as there is disturbing evidence that some physicians continue to perform and document brain-death determinations inadequately, standardizing optimum practices for physicians in determining death in DCD patients is clearly desirable. We should work toward developing an evidence based, optimum practice standard for determining death in DCD." For another representative example of the call for greater standardization of DCDD protocols, see Sonny Dhanani et al., "Survey of Determination of Death after Cardiac Arrest by Intensive Care Physicians," *Critical*

There is only one reason such a call for standardization makes sense: to reflect actual, or ontological, death. Otherwise, why would variability in the duration of circulatory arrest really matter? In other words, if extracting organs from donors in DCDD protocols is permissible when they incipiently are dying but not actually dead, then why would it matter if the harvesting begins at five, three, or two minutes; seventy-five seconds; or even, as some have proposed, prior to withdrawing life support.[60]

Physicians from the Netherlands wrote a letter to the editor of *Pediatric Critical Care Medicine* objecting to the two-minute waiting period at the US hospital of the authors of an earlier article. In turn, they stated their view that five minutes is sufficient. In the ensuing commentary, the original authors responded that their choice of a two-minute interval comported with accepted guidelines and pointed out that even a "5-min waiting period is not sufficient to establish irreversible loss of function of the entire brain, including the brain stem."[61]

Care Medicine 40.5 (May 2012): 1449–1455, doi: 10.1097 /CCM.0b013e31823e9898.

60. Paul Morrissey, "Kidney Donation from Brain-Injured Patients before a Declaration of Death," *Lahey Clinic Journal of Medical Ethics* 17.1 (Winter 2010): 1–2, 8.

61. Yorick J. de Groot and Erwin J.O. Kompanje, "Dead Donor Rule and Organ Procurement," *Pediatric Critical Care Medicine* 11.2 (March 2010): 315, doi: 10.1097/PCC.0b013e3181c3150d, comment on Kristine M. Pleacher et al., "Impact of a Pediatric Donation after Cardiac Death Program," *Pediatric Critical Care*

It is telling that proponents of a two-minute waiting period appeal to existing guidelines for their rationale rather than to an objective standard that is sufficient to establish irreversibility. They correctly observe that even settling on five minutes likewise fails to establish irreversibility as part of their justification for electing to accept a shorter threshold, instead of allowing that fact to sway their decision accordingly.

Ontological Status versus Medical Standards

Bernat sees these lines of demarcation clearly: "Declaring death in a DCD donor highlights a distinction between the ontology of death, as we might call it, and medical practice."[62] In brain death determinations, medical practice and ontology coincide. In DCDD protocols, Bernat sides with prevailing medical practice for declaring death over the ontological status of the donor. But this line of argumentation shifts the goal posts. It is not the strict category of alive or dead that counts, but something else. As long as "something else" counts, pressure will probably keep mounting to include other criteria, such as patient prognosis and autonomy, which opens the door for more radical proposals.

"From a purely ontological perspective," Bernat concedes, "these patients are not unequivocally dead

Medicine 10.2 (March 2009): 166–170, doi: 10.1097 /PCC.0b013e318194800b.

62. James L. Bernat, "The Debate over Death Determination in DCD," *Hastings Center Report* 40.3 (May–June 2010): 3, doi: 10.1353/hcr.0.0258.

until their cessation of circulation is irreversible."[63] The ontological status of the patient, however, never should be dismissed even as extrinsic conditions—such as a do-not-resuscitate (DNR) order—may be ethically chosen and observed. Jason Eberl makes this argument with great clarity: "It seems absurd to conceive of one's status as a living or dead human person to be alterable so capriciously by another's moral decisions. I thus submit that extrinsic conditions of whatever sort should not play a role in determining whether a human person is alive or dead; rather, we must endeavor to rationally identify what *intrinsic active natural potentialities* are present, allowing these alone—or in concert with other relevant intrinsic properties—to define the substantial existence and essential nature of the individual in front of us."[64]

Gert also recognizes the inadequacy of the status quo: "Although no one wants to say so, we now have death by decision."[65] One implication of this death-by-decision standard is that patients in biologically identical states could be regarded differently.[66] Subordinating ontological and biological considerations makes the determination of death contingent on whether a patient has a DNR order and is an organ donor. Such contingencies are not inherent components of the determination of brain death.

---

63. Ibid.

64. Jason T. Eberl, "The Unactualized Potential of PVS Patients," *APA Newsletter on Philosophy and Medicine* 11.1 (Fall 2011): 16, original emphasis.

65. Bernard Gert, "Definition of Death," *APA Newsletter on Philosophy and Medicine* 9.1 (Fall 2009): 8.

66. Eberl, *Thomistic Principles and Bioethics*, 125.

These factors make it reasonable to conclude that DCDD protocols largely do not comport with the sound anthropology Pope St. John Paul II had in mind when endorsing the legitimacy of brain death. The difference is in how these two methods correspond to the facts, to the underlying biological and spiritual reality. Moral certainty is the necessary and sufficient condition for determining that a person is dead, and that requirement has not been adequately satisfied in current DCDD protocols. The medical authorities, in essence, have said as much.

Shaky Proposals

The justification for current DCDD protocols leads inexorably to an important question: If these protocols permit organ extraction based on the certainty of imminent death and the patient's (or proxy's) autonomy and consent, why would it necessarily be wrong to allow organ donation in other circumstances in which those variables obtain?

There is, it seems, only one way to thwart the expansion of those scenarios: the dead donor rule must be interpreted to mean that the donor must in fact be dead, and not simply that the act of organ extraction does not constitute an act of killing. Once we allow for exceptions, we lose a suitably objective safeguard or reference point by which to measure proposed protocols, which in the continuous quest to expand the donor pool, are certain to keep pushing the envelope.

DCDD usually is planned and occurs in the ICU. These protocols are referred to as *controlled* donation after circulatory determination of death, or cDCDD.

(The *c* is typically omitted.) Yet there are also quite bold *uncontrolled* protocols (uDCDD) in which organs may be obtained after cardiac arrest occurs unexpectedly outside the hospital. These are currently in place in only a few countries, such as the United States, Spain, and France.

The uDCDD protocols are fraught with even greater ethical hazards. For one thing, they use organ preservation techniques before it is known whether the patient had expressed a desire to become an organ donor and before family or surrogates could possibly assent. Taking such invasive action violates that very principle of consent generally deemed so sacrosanct. If, as many argue, some premortem procedures may be justified by the principle of double effect in a controlled ICU setting when consent has clearly been obtained, that principle does not apply to uncontrolled situations. Furthermore, such presumptuousness only undermines, if not directly contradicts, the notion that organ donation is a profound *gift* of self. Consequently, uDCDD emits an unseemly aura of plunder.

Moreover, patients in these situations are exposed to CPR. This necessitates a longer, but as yet undetermined, waiting period because well-documented cases of autoresuscitation have occurred after failed CPR. There are also indications that a novel range of other resuscitative techniques may benefit patients even after conventional resuscitation outside the hospital has failed. Growing evidence from several countries suggests that these "non-conventional resuscitation procedures," when combined with continuing CPR, "are associated with promising survival rates with good neurological outcomes ... after discharge from hospital." In short, a paramount concern is that, in these uncontrolled DCDD protocols, circulatory or neurological function might not be lost irreversibly when organs are retrieved.[67]

If the distinction between alive and dead no longer binds absolutely, then the point at which objections to organ procurement are honored will keep receding. Indeed, one of the objections to current DCDD protocols is that they may foster further slippery-slope scenarios. Justifications for new forms of donation will keep shifting opportunistically, balancing the gravity of the donor's condition against the needs of prospective recipients.

Paul Morrissey of Brown University issued a controversial proposal that would allow *both* kidneys to be taken from a prospective DCDD candidate *before* life-sustaining therapy is withdrawn.[68] The justification for this particular proposal goes like this: After life support is withdrawn, the patient in a DCDD scenario ultimately dies from respiratory arrest caused by the original, massive brain injury. Withdrawing life support in this scenario is not an act of killing. Once this decision has been made, stripping the donor of his organs will not kill him, because he will die from his original condition before he dies as a consequence of having no kidneys. Bernat seems to countenance this proposal—at least he maintains that it does not violate the dead donor rule.[69]

---

67. David Rodríguez-Arias and Iván Ortega Deballon, "Protocols for Uncontrolled Donation after Circulatory Death," *Lancet* 379.9823 (April 7–13, 2012): 1275, doi: 10.1016/S0140-6736(11)61784-4.

68. Morrissey, "Kidney Donation," 1–2.

69. James L. Bernat, "Life or Death for the Dead-Donor Rule?," *New England Journal of Medicine* 369.14 (October 3, 2013): 1289–1297, doi: 10.1056/NEJMp1308078.

Several practical considerations make this controversial. Some patients could die during surgery, which could make it an act of killing. There is the risk that the severity of the underlying neurological injury could be inaccurately diagnosed. Furthermore, it is not clear how long any individual will live after life support is withdrawn; some fail to become donors precisely because they do not die soon enough.[70]

But suppose for the sake of argument that such a proposal constitutes, as Bernat puts it, "A type of living organ donation that does not kill the donor."[71] The same could well be said of current DCDD protocols that do not correspond with ontological death, that is, in which the donor is not yet known to be dead when death is pronounced. Consistency would seem to demand approval for any proposals fitting that profile.

Some Catholic scholars consider current DCDD protocols to be ethical because "even if the patient is still alive, extracting his organs (perhaps including his heart, if it is viable) will not hasten his death. Here death is not intended, either as an end or as a means. Not only that, one does not even cause or hasten the patient's death as a side effect; one does not cause or hasten his death at

_____

70. For an effective rebuttal of Morrissey's proposal, see Wesley J. Smith, "Killing for Organs: Doctor Says Take Neurologically Devastated Patients' Kidneys before They Are Dead," Center for Bioethics and Culture, www.cbc -network.org. Smith convincingly argues that such a proposal treats the person as an object, which is harmful both to the person and to society, and that accepting its logic would leads to other such objectification and abuses.

71. Bernat, "Life or Death," 1289.

all."[72] If this view prevails, it will make the causation and hastening of death, rather than death itself, the determining factor and core requirements of the dead donor rule. That seems to be a more malleable standard. We are left, then, to ponder whether any proposal which "uncouples organ donation from the donor's death,"[73] as Morrissey honestly describes his model, is ethically licit. If so, under what conditions and by recourse to which principles?

---

72. Patrick Lee and Robert P. George, *Body–Self Dualism in Contemporary Ethics and Politics* (Cambridge, UK: Cambridge University Press, 2008), 169.

73. Morrissey, "Kidney Donation," 1.

7

Relevant Principles of Living Donation

Current practice surrounding donation after circulatory determination of death, along with more aggressive proposals to permit patients facing imminent death to donate their organs, forces us to identify the principles that render some forms of organ transplantation from living donors permissible and others impermissible. Bernat has cautioned that DCDD might manipulate dying patients, and its ethical justification remains unsettled within the medical community.[1] It is also a matter that the Church has not explicitly addressed. Catholic

---

1. James L. Bernat and Nathaniel M. Robbins, "How Should Physicians Manage Organ Donation after the Circulatory Determination of Death in Patients with Extremely Poor Neurological Prognosis?," *AMA Journal of Ethics* 20.8 (August 2018): 708–716, doi: 10.1001/amajethics.2018.708. The authors write, "An unresolved ethical question is whether and how donor consent should be seen as authorizing manipulation of a living donor during the dying process solely for to benefit of the organ recipient" (708).

teaching with respect to the ethics of organ donation has developed considerably over time; the very act of living donation, once shunned but now sanctioned, has been a matter of extensive debate.

On what grounds is it proper to give some part of one's body for the sake of another person? After all, the body has a profound integrity of its own, and it is not to be mutilated. A diseased portion of the body may be removed if doing so preserves the life of the whole person. Conversely, it would not be permissible to remove, say, a perfectly healthy leg. Although rare, some people actually wish to amputate a healthy limb—a condition now termed body integrity identity disorder.[2]

Pope Pius XII specified that removing part of oneself may be justified to preserve the good of the whole person: "By virtue of the principle of totality, by virtue of his right to use the services of his organism as a whole, the patient can allow individual parts to be destroyed or mutilated when and to the extent necessary for the good of his being as a whole." But he did so with binding limits in mind: "As for the patient, he is not absolute master of himself, of his body or of his soul. He cannot, therefore, freely dispose of himself as he pleases. Even the reason for which he acts is of itself neither sufficient nor determining."[3]

---

2. Robert Song, "Body Integrity Identity Disorder and the Ethics of Mutilation," *Studies in Christian Ethics* 26.4 (November 2013): 490, doi: 10.1177/0953946813492921.

3. Pius XII, *The Moral Limits of Medical Research and Treatment* (1952), n. 13, available at http://www.papalencyclicals.net/.

But could a healthy organ be removed from a living person not for his own sake, but for the sake of another person? According to the influential Jesuit Gerald Kelly, this cannot be justified by the principle of totality. In the early 1950s, totality was being proposed as a justifying principle: if humanity as a whole could be interpreted as a metaphor for a single body—parts of which could be sacrificed for the good of the whole—then the principle of totality, which justifies removal of a body part for the sake of that person, could be invoked to justify the removal of a body part from one person for the sake of another.

Subordinating a part for the sake of the whole applies within one's own physical body, but it does not have wider societal application: "Totality," Kelly wrote, "is essentially a principle of subordination of part to whole—a subordination which exists only in a physical body, not in a moral body or even in the Mystical Body. Catholic teaching, as expressed particularly in the pronouncements of Pius XII, has constantly denied this subordination of a person to society."[4]

But Kelly felt that living donation could be justified by appealing to charity, as Bert Cunningham first proposed in the 1940s.[5] Making a distinction between an ordinary rule and its exceptions, Kelly judged that "the basis for the opinion favoring organic transplantation would be stated as follows: 'Ordinarily, direct

4. Gerald Kelly, "The Morality of Mutilation: Towards a Revision of the Treatise," *Theological Studies* 17.3 (September 1956): 332–333.

5. For a brief discussion of this history, see William E. May, *Catholic Bioethics and the Gift of Human Life*, 2nd ed. (Huntingdon, IN: Our Sunday Visitor, 2008), 355.

self-mutilation is permitted only for one's own good; but in exceptional cases the law of charity allows it for the benefit of the neighbor.'"[6]

Just what constitutes "exceptional cases" remains ambiguous. But surely this exceptionality cannot be regarded as overlapping precisely with the overall need for transplants at any given time. Otherwise, the principle of charity could be invoked to sanction progressively expansive donation protocols.

One tension pertaining to this argument concerns the question of what precisely constitutes mutilation. *Veritatis splendor* listed mutilation as an intrinsically evil act, and there are, after all, no exceptions to rules pertaining to intrinsically evil acts. Some theologians feel that living donation cannot properly be said to involve mutilation at all, whereas others feel that organ donation and transplantation simply cannot be done without mutilation.[7]

Ultimately, by recourse to charity, the view that one could preserve one's overall bodily integrity *and* be a living donor prevailed, provided that one's functional integrity remained intact. In other words, a person could sacrifice *anatomical* integrity in certain situations for the sake of another, as long as this would not compromise the *functional* integrity of the donor. Some have found support for this conclusion in the fact that the *Catechism*

---

6. Kelly, "Morality of Mutilation," 342.

7. Anthony Stoeppel and Pablo Requena, "Organ Donation Is Not Mutilation: The History of an Erroneous Idea," *National Catholic Bioethics Quarterly* 13.3 (Autumn 2013): 427–436.

of the Catholic Church specifies that it is *disabling* mutilation that is objectionable.[8]

So, a living donor may give a single kidney but not two because the donor can still function normally with only one kidney. This would not apply to, say, a cornea; although we have two eyes, we need both to see normally. A living person, therefore, may not donate a cornea even with a genuinely altruistic motive.

With this distinction in mind, a key question presents itself: What does the functional integrity of a person really mean in the context of controlled DCDD scenarios, assuming the donor is in the final moments of life but not yet dead—or even at the moment life support is withdrawn and the donor is clearly still alive? The very fact that imminent death is foreseen with great confidence suggests that one's very "functioning" is known to be fading and soon will never return.

Therefore, the concept of functional integrity lends itself, at least in theory, to living donation once it has been established that the donor's own capacity to maintain function will not be jeopardized by the organ's removal. Yet the living person still retains a great dignity and bodily integrity which is to be respected.

Paul Morrissey's proposal to extract both kidneys prior to withdrawing life support essentially relies on the same argument, albeit with different terminology, that the donor's functional integrity is no longer at issue, because of his proximity with death.[9] With such a short

---

8. Ibid.

9. Paul Morrissey, "Kidney Donation from Brain-Injured Patients before a Declaration of Death," *Lahey Clinic Journal of Medical Ethics* 17.1 (Winter 2010): 1.

amount of life remaining, the dying donor does not really *need* those organs to possess functional integrity. With this understanding, one could also proceed to take the corneas of the dying donor because this procedure will neither kill him nor affect his functional integrity. He will soon be dead and therefore not need to see. One might even argue that most organ removal at this stage would not technically constitute a "disabling" mutilation. Anything that does not directly kill the donor or cause harm would be fair game.

By this reading, functional integrity could even be invoked to countenance the extraction of organs from anencephalic infants, at least when they are known to be nearing death. Based on their condition at birth, we cannot expect them to survive for long; they simply lack the capacity to function with ordinary persistence. Like in DCDD scenarios, the arrival of death is only a matter of time.

Something else, something beyond one's capacity to function, must also be respected, according to clear indications from the magisterium: "It is obvious," Pope St. John Paul II stressed in 1991, "that vital organs can only be donated *after death*." [10] Again in 2000, he emphasized that "*vital organs which occur singly in the body can be removed only after death*, that is from the body of someone who is certainly dead." [11] Pope Benedict XVI

10. John Paul II, Address to participants of the First International Congress of the Society for Organ Sharing (June 20, 1991), n. 4, original emphasis.

11. John Paul II, Address to the eighteenth International Congress of the Transplantation Society (August 29, 2000), n. 4, original emphasis.

was also emphatic about this point, stressing that "the principal criteria of respect for the life of the donor must always prevail so that the extraction of organs be performed only in the case of his/her true death."[12]

It seems reasonable to conclude that this requirement would also apply to DCDD protocols and the extraction of two kidneys from a donor while still alive but nearing death. Otherwise, one might also arguably be permitted to donate non-paired organs once death by another cause is foreseen. In any event, there have been no authoritative indications that living donation is acceptable, provided that it does not constitute an act of direct killing. We are required to wait for the moment of death even if it is obviously, permissibly, and incontrovertibly foreseen. Functionality is therefore not the decisive consideration, suggesting that even the most sincere appeal to charity does not always carry the day when it comes to procuring organs and tissues.

Finality and Charity

Reflecting on the theological developments over the past century with respect to the permissibility of living transplantation, moral theologian Janet Smith has raised important considerations. Smith goes back to Pope Pius XI (*Casti connubii*) and from there traces how the principles of finality, totality, and charity have been interpreted in the magisterium and by other influential

---

12. Benedict XVI, Address to participants at an international congress organized by the Pontifical Academy for Life (November 7, 2008).

theologians with contrasting views. Pius XII, she convincingly argues,

> "repeatedly taught that LOT [organ transplantation from living donor] violated what came to be called the principle of finality, the principle that the parts of one's body have as their natural *telos* the good of one's body only and have no other *telos*: to give one's organs to another suggests that one's bodily parts are ordered not just to one's own good but to the good of another. In his view, the principle of finality ruled out the possibility of the use of the principle of totality to justify LOT." [13]

She acknowledges that others, including Paul Ramsey, argued that a living donor acts not only to benefit another, but also to benefit himself because his free act is virtuous, and virtue by definition is beneficial to the one who performs it. Yet she maintains that "it was the principle of finality that was most definitive in [Pius XII's] reasoning," and he "did not accept the principle of charity as justifying LOT." [14]

She also notes that living donation was approved and practiced in Catholic hospitals here in the United States even as Pius XII spoke against it; John Paul II did provide the first magisterial endorsement of living donation, but that was not until 1984.

Another theologian, Rev. Stephen Torraco, has maintained that moral theology has accomplished very

---

13. Janet E. Smith, "Organ Transplants: A Study on Bioethics and the Ordinary Magisterium," in *The Ethics of Organ Transplantation*, ed. Steven J. Jensen (Washington, DC: Catholic University of America Press, 2011), 280–281.

14. Ibid., 288, 289.

little between the times of Pius XII and John Paul II. Since both *Gaudium et spes* and *Veritatis splendor* refer to mutilation as an intrinsic evil, the only operational justification for the practice of living donation has consisted of an appeal to the motive of charity. But Torraco stresses that "a good *why* (even charity)... cannot make a bad *what* good."[15] The distinction between functional and anatomical integrity, in his view, only "sideskirts" the deepest questions concerning the meaning and value of the embodied human person.

The practice of (limited) living donation has become commonplace today because, ultimately, the thought of several influential theologians gained wide acceptance; the current understanding is that the principle of totality may not be invoked to justify living donation, but charity can as long as functional integrity is not imperiled.

But if charity and functional integrity are always the two decisive considerations, it would seem to allow one to break with a strict interpretation of the dead donor rule. In cases of living donation when death is foreseeably imminent, to speak of one's *functional* integrity makes less sense; if charity justifies organ donation from healthy donors with that one proviso, why can it not also justify donation from dying donors as long as that same proviso is satisfied? It is not a stretch to suppose that the charity of the donor could be the same in each case, as could be the lack of peril to one's functional integrity.

---

15. Stephen F. Torraco, "*Veritatis Splendor* and the Ethics of Organ Transplants," *Linacre Quarterly* 64.2 (May 1997): 52.

Finality was once understood as the cornerstone, the foundational principle governing all transplantation-related considerations involving living donors; it propelled the Church to insist that certain forms of donation are acceptable only if they occur after death. It therefore seems as though appealing to charity to justify living donation may well have a limited application even though it has gained widespread acceptance in "normal" circumstances. At present, it seems fair to conclude that the Church teaches that charity may override finality in some but not all scenarios.

In light of these lingering tensions, Smith concludes, "I believe a Church document laying out the principles behind the approval of LOT and addressing many of the collateral issues is long overdue and would be very beneficial."[16] Such clarification would seem to be even more urgent in light of the current DCDD protocols—which may be said to constitute an act of living donation if the donor is not dead at the moment the procedure commences—and in light of more explicitly radical procedures such as the one proposed by Morrissey. Approval of these procedures would seem to further erode the principle of finality and acquiesce to a particular interpretation of charity.

The Requirement of Establishing Death

The importance of drawing a clear line in the sand and adhering to it is hard to overstate. For instance, Scott

---

16. Smith, "Organ Transplants," 302.

Halpern, a physician at the University of Pennsylvania, is far from alone in his desire to dispense with the dead donor rule; he feels that patient autonomy and beneficence should override our "servility" to the rule. If his favored principles were to be adopted with transparency, the need for certainty about whether patients are actually dead at the time of donation would evaporate. The data we now have (and may reasonably expect to obtain in the foreseeable future), he notes, are not robust enough to vindicate current DCDD protocols. He therefore gathers, in a manner that demonstrates both his logic as well as his dissatisfaction, that our current "servility to the dead-donor-rule also means that we cannot justify DCDD of any kind." [17]

Some other commentators, also representing prestigious institutions, have pounced on the overall ambiguities and inconsistencies in death determination to explicitly argue that killing should be permitted. They maintain that death as determined by either the neurological criteria or the DCDD standard does not correspond to actual death, meaning that all organ transplantation amounts to killing; however, instead of concluding that vital-organ extraction may not be performed on living donors, they maintain it is all acceptable because every donor, although still alive, is "totally disabled." With respect to DCDD protocols employing a two- to five–minute waiting period, they do incisively assert that "consistency with traditional medical ethics

---

17. Scott D. Halpern, "Donation after Circulatory Determination of Death: Time for Transparency," *Annals of Emergency Medicine* 63.4 (April 2014): 402, doi: 10.1016/j.annemergmed.2013.09.020.

would entail that this kind of vital organ donation must cease immediately." From that premise, they nevertheless proceed to write that "luckily," the need to respect the dead donor rule "is easily obviated by abandoning the norm against killing."[18]

Dismissing the prohibition against active killing is obviously a nonstarter. The question remains, however, Does being dead or alive really matter? And why? If the principle of charity permits the donation of a single kidney because it does not affect the donor's functional integrity, why can't it also justify the donation of multiple organs prior to death when that act will likewise not adversely affect the donor's functional integrity?

The scenarios John Paul II had in mind (pertaining, say, to a healthy, living kidney donor) when pronouncing favorably on some forms of living donation are clear enough, whereas the application of the relevant principles in the context of DCDD remains murky at best. Given that living donation is considered licit precisely because it amounts to a freely chosen act of donation, rather than mutilation, requiring death to be established (a strict interpretation of the dead donor rule) essentially exposes the inherent tension between the principles of charity and finality; it ultimately amounts to a nod to finality.

There are a couple of competing approaches to living donation that may not constitute a direct act of killing. On the one hand, Rev. Nicanor Austriaco

---

18. Walter Sinnott-Armstrong and Franklin G. Miller, "What Makes Killing Wrong?," *Journal of Medical Ethics* 39.1 (January 2013): 6, 7, doi: 10.1136/medethics-2011 -100351.

offers a thought-provoking proposal that forces us to think through the bedrock principles. With respect to DCDD protocols in general (not specifically the kind of proposal Morrissey has in mind), he writes that organ donation would be permissible once a person's organs are no longer "vital." He means after asystole, when respiration and circulation have ceased but before the donor has died. He regards the non-heart-beating donor in current DCDD protocols as still alive, but he feels that it "should be permissible for the still-living individual to donate his once, but no longer vital, organs as a last act of charity before his death."[19]

The motive here is easy to appreciate, but even this creative rationale nonetheless conflicts with the magisterium's clear indications that such procedures may occur only after death. Yet it is not immediately clear why it could not be justified if *mere* functional integrity is not compromised and if charity may truly be the overriding, operative principle in all such instances. Is invoking the principle of charity sufficient in these cases to offset the fact that the donor may be operated on before his or her death? If it is sufficient, is it sufficient for the properly disposed person acting out of an authentically charitable disposition, or is it more broadly sufficient as a matter of wise public policy?

Austriaco's fellow Dominican Rev. Romanus Cessario objects to the notion that transplantation fits smoothly into a classically Thomistic view of charity: "At best," he writes, "Thomists regard the transplantation

19. Nicanor Pier Giorgio Austriaco, *Biomedicine and Beatitude: An Introduction to Catholic Bioethics* (Washington, DC: Catholic University of America Press, 2011), 203.

of organs, whether from the living or the dead, as a free act of supererogation. They are eager also to restrain the rather loose use of the term 'charity'" that characterized much of the discussion on organ donation in the mid-twentieth century.[20]

He distinguishes between the "moral realism" and "order of charity" characteristic of Thomism and the prevailing but more metaphysically ambiguous notions of altruism and "ersatz 'charity.'"[21] The Church, he observes, has correctly refused to make organ donation a universal obligation of charity; he further maintains that on account of developments over the past several decades, it is unfortunate "that many suffer under the impression that the Church officially endorses organ donation as an exercise of true charity."[22]

Jason Eberl, it might be interjected here, concurs that it is not a requirement of charity, but he reaches the more favorable conclusion that "organ donation is a morally virtuous act that is strongly supported by the Thomistic natural law ethic, even if it is not morally or legally mandated."[23] John Paul II quite clearly felt that circumstances exist in which charity could prevail. In his 2000 address to the Transplantation Society, for

---

20. Romanus Cessario, "Organ Donation and the Beatific Vision: Thomist Moral Theology Confronts the Tide of Relativism," in Jensen, *Ethics of Organ Transplantation*, 197.

21. Ibid., 198, 212–213.

22. Ibid., 206. See also 211.

23. Jason T. Eberl, *Thomistic Principles and Bioethics* (New York: Routledge, 2006), 126.

example, he said that "every organ transplant has its source in a decision of great ethical value: 'the decision to offer without reward a part of one's own body for the health and well-being of another person.' Here precisely lies the nobility of the gesture, a gesture which is a genuine act of love."[24] Benedict XVI also deemed this gesture of donation to be "a peculiar form of witness to charity."[25]

Pius XII, as mentioned above, rejected the notion that charity could justify living donation; out of deference to developments in philosophical interpretation, Cessario does not challenge current Church teaching on the practice. (A parish priest, who later was appointed an auxiliary bishop of Dallas, donated a kidney to one of his parishioners.)[26] Yet Cessario argues that while the practice is permissible and "can be meritorious" as per the *Catechism*,[27] it is not ideal; it is to be hoped that one

---

24. John Paul II, Address to the Transplantation Society, n. 3, citing his address to the Society for Organ Sharing, n. 3.

25. Benedict XVI, address to the Pontifical Academy for Life.

26. Catholic World News, "New US Bishop Donated Kidney to Parishioner," CatholicCulture.org, March 12, 2010, https://www.catholicculture.org/.

27. *Catechism*, n. 2296. "*Organ transplants* are in conformity with the moral law if the physical and psychological dangers and risks to the donor are proportionate to the good sought for the recipient. Organ donation after death is a noble and meritorious act and is to be encouraged as an expression of generous solidarity. It is not morally acceptable if the donor or his proxy has not given explicit consent. Moreover, it is not morally admissible to bring

day other measures may become available and render organ transplantation unnecessary.

In support of his contention, Cessario cites Benedict XVI's 2008 address to the Pontifical Academy for Life in which he expressed hope that new approaches and advances would render current organ transplantation practices obsolete. That address, like Church teaching generally in this area, Cessario characterizes as follows: "Cautious reserve not enthusiasm marks these texts." Amidst the competing tensions currently being balanced, Cessario firmly maintains that "one thing is clear: the Church is not ready to enshrine organ donation permanently among the corporal works of mercy."[28]

Deeper Considerations

Airing competing views such as these seems healthy, particularly as some of the most profound questions are rarely asked, because of the pressing pursuit of transplantable organs. Gilbert Meilaender, a theologian and former member of the President's Council on Bioethics (PCBE), has observed that we are reluctant to think through the deeper questions about our bodies and lives because this "may raise disquieting questions about organ transplantation generally."[29] It is easier to let fundamental questions take a back seat and focus on meeting present exigencies. One thing we wish to avoid

---

about the disabling mutilation or death of a human being, even in order to delay the death of other persons."

28. Cessario, "Organ Donation," 199, 200.

29. Gilbert Meilaender, "Gifts of the Body," *New Atlantis* no. 13 (Summer 2006): 26.

contemplating, he contends, is that the reality of the dignity of the embodied person is so compelling that it is hard to see why even gifts of the body, to say nothing of sales of the body, should be permitted.

Another unsettling aspect of transplantation—that a surgeon should operate on one person for the benefit of another—has not gone away despite the "now widely shared presumption" that donation is not only morally acceptable but praiseworthy. Meilaender, like many others, wonders how, in a span of a few short decades, we have gone from the clear pronouncements of Pius XI and Pius XII against such invasive procedures—except to benefit the individual—to the more favorable stance espoused by John Paul II. Chief among Meilaender's carefully reasoned misgivings is the question, to what extent is transplantation a manifestation of our having come to treat death as a problem to be solved? [30]

Ultimately, Meilaender, like John Paul II, finds justification for organ transplantation only in the sense that it is a gift. Still, we are faced with the question, are there some gifts (parts of our bodies) we may not give while we are still alive, even if we are disposed to do so by virtue of our sincere generosity? Meilaender concludes that this justification must have limits as well: "Even when we override it for very important reasons, bodily integrity continues to be a great good that cannot simply be ignored in our deliberations. It continues to exert moral pressure, and, if it permits some gifts of the body, it does not permit any and all." [31]

---

30. Ibid., 28, 29.
31. Ibid., 35.

He is adamant that we need to heed the "deep-seated and legitimate reasons for hesitation about organ transplantation." In failing to recognize them, and by focusing solely on how to rectify the shortage of available organs, "death itself becomes a kind of technicality—an obstacle to organ procurement, which obstacle must be surmounted in order to procure the body's parts and accomplish our worthy purposes." As a result, he concludes, we risk losing something very important: a humane death. That steep price applies across the board—that is, by whatever criteria are used—but he does single out the DCDD protocols that essentially "plan the deaths of patients" and are clearly driven "by a supposed imperative to diminish an organ shortage."[32]

At some level, this notion of a shortage—that demand for organs exceeds their supply, a staple of the scientific literature—conflicts with the concept of organ donation as gift, which the Church insists on as a nonnegotiable prerequisite for procurement. It is not uncommon for this shortage to be described as a "national crisis." Yet would it not be regarded as unseemly or presumptuous to talk about the "shortage" of other kinds of gifts?

The President's Council on Bioethics on DCDD

The PCBE also weighed in on the determination of death by the circulatory criteria in the context of organ donation. Primarily because of the requirement that circulatory and respiratory arrest must be irreversible,

---

32. Ibid., 32, 35.

it too found DCDD protocols to be more troubling than brain death protocols.

The council goes a step further in asserting that, the issue of irreversibility aside, there is still an ethical dilemma inherent in the procedure itself because it necessarily entails hurrying: "There is reason to worry that this practice—if carried out on a wide scale—could make the donor's death seem like a mere formality, with 'patient dies' becoming simply another item to check off on a list of events required for a successful controlled DCDD procurement. ... Rushing to make a declaration as quickly as possible is not viewed as respectful or appropriate. Unfortunately, such a deliberate demeanor is harder to maintain if the death is going to be 'made use of' for the sake of other needy patients."[33]

It seems as though these concerns would remain legitimate even if this practice were not carried out on a wide scale. Some recent findings are not reassuring. According to a 2011 survey, approximately 9 percent of the participating hospitals in one organ procurement region did not even permit families to be present from the time treatment was withdrawn until the moment of death.[34] Beyond the fact that families should be told

---

33. President's Council on Bioethics, *Controversies in the Determination of Death* (December 2008), 86, available at https://repository.library.georgetown.edu/bitstream/handle/10822/559343/Controversies%20in%20the%20Determination%20of%20Death%20for%20the%20Web.pdf?sequence=1&isAllowed=y.

34. J. Y. Rhee et al., "The Impact of Variation in Donation after Cardiac Death Policies among Donor Hospitals: A Regional Analysis," *American Journal of Transplantation*

that the interpretation of *irreversibility* is contested and that DCDD protocols may well disrupt the process of mourning at the bedside, the PCBE recommends that there should be additional public debate over whether DCDD should be standard practice. With respect to the moral warrant for declaring death, they maintain that the current framework, which requires consent and the impossibility of autoresuscitation, satisfies the necessary conditions, but these alone "may or may not be *sufficient*."[35]

If that position were to be evaluated according to the anthropological and philosophical benchmark used by John Paul II, it would appear that the PCBE has concluded that these protocols do not establish the donor's death with moral certainty. Having arrived at that verdict, however, the council stopped short of recommending any particular corrective measures.

The Organ Procurement Transplantation Network

A creeping laxity is perhaps to be expected in the absence of measures to counter the inexorable pressure that the "shortage" of organs exerts on ethical safeguards. We only have to turn to the Organ Procurement

---

11.8 (August 2011): 1721, doi: 10.1111/j.1600-6143 .2011.03634.x.

35. PCBE, *Controversies in the Determination of Death*, 86, 87, original emphasis.

and Transplantation Network (OPTN) for an example. In recent years, the OPTN has attempted to loosen the policy governing DCDD protocols, labeling its proposed alterations as a "plain language rewrite." The language, however, is anything but clear. For example, in evaluating a potential donor's suitability, the OPTN proposes that the patient has, among other things, a "non-recoverable" neurological injury, but non-recoverable is not defined. Such imprecise criteria could be interpreted to include even a conscious patient whose injury is neither progressive nor end-stage.

Another major concern is that the revised language does not specifically prohibit the evaluation of donor suitability before the patient or surrogate makes an independent decision to withdraw life support. The proposed revisions would even allow the evaluation to take place without the patient's (or surrogate's) knowledge, consent, or authorization. This would amount to a clear abuse of privacy and informed consent. Furthermore, such a violation undermines the whole concept of organ donation as gift. Another glaring omission is the absence of a required waiting period following cardiac arrest before death can be determined. This opens up the possibility that death could be determined in a capricious manner, without reasonable and appropriate safeguards.

These are among the significant and problematic alterations that undermine the OPTN's claim that its proposed revision "does not make any substantive changes to the content of the current Policies, but only changes the current language to make it easier to understand with more consistent terminology, better organization, and new usability features, including a table of contents."[36] The revisions, in fact, seriously weaken the protections afforded by the dead donor rule and informed consent.

Duplicity emanating from the authorities is never a good sign. When it is coupled with a federal mandate that every hospital must adopt DCDD policies, there is even greater cause for concern. Some Catholic bioethicists have reached the overall conclusion that the ambiguities and shortcuts advanced by the OPTN threaten to preclude Catholic participation in organ procurement.[37]

Possible Solutions

As it stands now, more than two decades after DCDD protocols were introduced, the issue at the center of the controversy—are the donors alive or dead—remains unresolved, despite extensive debate. DCDD protocols have been mainstreamed, despite lack of resolution, because, as Bernat explains, the "medical standard" of determining death has prevailed over the biological standard—that is, a standard of permanence has prevailed over a standard of irreversibility. The standard of permanence, which reflects the evolution of Bernat's perspective, has been met mainly by public acceptance: "There is neither a public outcry over it nor calls to

---

36. Organ Procurement Transplantation Network, *At a Glance: OPTN Policy Plain Language Rewrite*, cited in Marie T. Hilliard, letter to John Roberts, President, Board of Directors, OPTN, September 9, 2013, available at https://www.ncbcenter.org/.

37. Ibid.

abandon it, although," he adds with admirable fairness, "the public is probably mostly unaware of the practice."[38]

The authors of the opposing view published alongside Bernat's hold that "the absence of a public outcry can hardly be considered evidence of societal acceptance for a position that is surrounded by complexity, confusion, and lack of transparency." They even suspect that Bernat is not quite convinced that the permanence standard suffices: "Rejecting the use of [extracorporeal membrane oxygenation] is evidence, in our view, that one is uncomfortable with permanence alone."[39]

A certain awareness that different standards are in effect for the neurological and circulatory criteria can also be detected in the 2014 guidelines developed by an expert panel in collaboration with the World Health Organization. In describing the neurological sequence of events leading to death, the panel refers to a stage at which "brain function could return spontaneously or be restored through intervention." Death, they are careful to specify, cannot be established at that stage. It is only later (assuming all other variables are satisfied), when "the brain has ceased functioning and there is no possibility to resume," that death may be determined.

---

38. James L. Bernat, "On the Noncongruence between the Concept and Determination of Death," *Hastings Center Report* 43.6 (November–December 2013): 28 doi: 10.1002/hast.231.

39. David Rodríguez-Arias and Carissa Véliz, "The Death Debates: A Call for Public Deliberation," *Hastings Center Report* 43.6 (November–December 2013): 34, 35, doi: 10.1002/hast.232.

Since irreversibility is established, they simply write, "The patient has died."[40]

In contrast, when referring to the circulatory sequence that leads to death, the threshold and language are different. The authors refer to the stage at which it is known that, as long as no external intervention takes place, "cessation of breathing and circulation is permanent and the patient *may be determined to be dead*."[41] It is one thing to say that a patient has died, and another to say that a patient may be determined to be dead. The former is factual and expressed with confidence; the latter is equivocal and context dependent.

Although he advocates for a standard of permanence, Bernat nonetheless acknowledges that "compelling and reasoned arguments" have consistently challenged this view. A policy decision must be made in favor of either the medical practice standard of permanence or the biological standard of irreversibility: "Ultimately," he maintains, "policymakers must choose which type of death determination for organ donors works best for society."[42] That is the question before us: Should this ongoing discrepancy be acceptable?

---

40. Sam D. Shemie et al., "International Guideline Development for the Determination of Death," *Intensive Care Medicine* 40.6 (June 2014): 791, doi: 10.1007/s00134-014-3242-7.

41. Ibid., 794, emphasis added.

42. James L. Bernat, "On the Debate over Death Determination in Organ Donors," *Annals of Emergency Medicine* 63.4 (April 2014): 497, doi: 10.1016/j.annemergmed.2013.12.006.

The Church probably would support this type of organ donation *provided* the donor's death can be established. Eberl contends that a ten- to fifteen-minute waiting period after asystole is sufficient.[43] Since no current DCDD protocols in the United States have such a sufficient waiting period, an impasse is conspicuously evident.

It would be difficult for Catholic institutions to reconcile their practices with a standard other than actual death. The Catholic Church has made no specific statements about DCDD protocols, and the *Ethical and Religious Directives for Catholic Health Care Services* have not taken any specific position on them.[44]

In 2003, the Archdiocese of St. Louis did call for a moratorium on and a reevaluation of DCDD protocols in St. Louis hospitals.[45] That recommendation failed to gain much traction. In 2004, a physician and a Jesuit coauthored a medical-ethical analysis. They concluded that there appears to be a medically feasible and ethically permissible solution but that the status quo is problematic. They stressed that the ambiguities and

---

43. Eberl, *Thomistic Principles and Bioethics*, 126.

44. Peter A. Clark and Uday Deshmukh, "Non-heart-beating Organ Donation and Catholic Ethics," *National Catholic Bioethics Quarterly* 4.3 (Autumn 2004): 540.

45. Nancy Valko, "Organ Donation: Crossing the Line," *MercatorNet*, October 6, 2011, https://www.mercatornet .com/.

inconsistencies in DCDD protocols should preclude their use in Catholic health care facilities.[46]

It is unclear why that position has not been more widely adopted or even if it has been formally considered. Few Catholic institutions seem to have explicitly distanced themselves from current DCDD protocols. Perhaps this reflects a lack of official, concrete guidance on this particular issue; perhaps some institutions feel invested in the good of organ transplantation; or perhaps other issues have been more highly prioritized.

In any event, discomfort with DCDD protocols has persisted and escalated, even as they have become more entrenched. In a recent survey of health practitioners' attitudes and beliefs in the United States, Spain, and France, respondents clearly expressed the view that the brain death determination is more reliable than the circulatory determination. Consistent with that belief, the vast majority also expressed the view that organ donation from brain-dead donors is morally permissible, but that it is "much more controversial" in DCDD protocols. The authors' recommendation, however, was limited to clarifying and addressing the sources of practitioners' discomfort.[47] In contrast, another international team

---

46. Clark and Deshmukh, "Non-heart-beating Organ Donation," 550.

47. David Rodríguez-Arias et al., "One or Two Types of Death? Attitudes of Health Professionals towards Brain Death and Donation after Circulatory Death in Three Countries," *Medicine, Health Care, and Philosophy* 16.3 (July 2013): 457, doi: 10.1007/s11019-011-9369-1.

of practitioners, having examined these same issues in 2011, called for a moratorium on DCDD.[48]

The more commonly held position seems to be that DCDD protocols should continue in their present form while efforts are made to achieve greater standardization in guidelines and uniformity in practice through public, medical, and political dialogue. An example of this viewpoint can be found in a 2012 article in *Critical Care Medicine*, which discusses a survey of Canadian adult and pediatric intensive care physicians who had experience in making death determinations following cardiac arrest. Physicians reported "wide variability in reported practice," as well as instances of autoresuscitation. In fact, 37 percent of respondents reported having witnessed a case themselves, and 81 percent indicated the phenomenon merited further study.[49] There was also strong agreement among the respondents that standardization is needed, especially in the context of organ donation.

These are key issues, yet this survey did not explicitly address the pivotal question of the waiting period required to ensure irreversibility. In fact, that central consideration never really surfaced in the analysis. The

---

48. Ari R. Joffe et al., "Donation after Cardiocirculatory Death: A Call for a Moratorium pending Full Public Disclosure and Fully Informed Consent," *Philosophy, Ethics, and Humanities in Medicine* 6 (2011): 1–20, doi: 10.1186/1747-5341-6-17.

49. Sonny Dhanani et al., "Survey of Determination of Death after Cardiac Arrest by Intensive Care Physicians," *Critical Care Medicine* 40.5 (May 2012): 1451, 1452, doi: 10.1097/CCM.0b013e31823e9898.

authors emphasized that the potential for autoresuscitation in some cases is a chief area of concern, since it raises doubts about the irreversibility of circulatory arrest. True as this statement is, it also evades the fact that irreversibility is not yet established once autoresuscitation becomes impossible, as long as it still remains physiologically possible to reverse the process of dying by external means. It would appear that focusing on autoresuscitation alone (as in this survey) reflects a prior commitment to current protocols based on permanence rather than irreversibility.

Halting or Adjusting Current DCDD Practice

The alternative to maintaining the status quo while seeking improvements, of course, is to prohibit DCDD until the necessary and sufficient conditions for death have been established. Ari Joffe and colleagues presented a detailed rationale for this position.[50] Their comprehensive critique extends beyond concern about violating the dead donor rule to other aspects of DCDD protocols, such as conflicts of interest and the use of premortem interventions which are designed primarily for the benefit of the recipient and not of the donor.

The latter are serious issues that, if not properly managed, may indeed present occasions for abuse. That is not to say, however, that these issues represent categorical obstacles. Conversely, every violation of the dead donor rule does represent a breach of ethical practice. Several Catholic scholars have argued persuasively that it is

---

50. Joffe et al., "Donation after Cardiocirculatory Death," 1–20.

possible, by observing proper safeguards, to avoid conflicts of interest and to licitly administer premortem agents. Even if every other aspect of the DCDD process is flawlessly performed, however, the status of the donor (alive or dead) must always be established.

Another group of physicians, led by Joseph Carcillo, called for a suspension of current DCDD practices. Citing a 2008 survey indicating that most pediatricians are not confident that the DCDD donor is actually dead, they offered a sketch of their rationale as to why the practice should be halted. One reason they provided, however, has been subject to critique. They referred to the potential for autoresuscitation (the "Lazarus phenomenon") after more than five to ten minutes of asystole. Although this has occurred among patients who had received prior attempts at resuscitation which were thought to have failed, it has never occurred among patients who were withdrawn from life support. Nevertheless, they are correct to take irreversibility to mean "a state that cannot be reversed, whether we choose to try to reverse it or not." In their view, this fundamental consideration simply should not be evaded.[51]

Their call for a moratorium garnered a pointed response from several other pediatric intensivists, who

---

51. Joseph A. Carcillo et al., "A Call for Full Public Disclosure and Moratorium on Donation after Cardiac Death in Children," *Pediatric Critical Care Medicine* 11.5 (September 2010): 641–643, doi: 10.1097/PCC.0b013e3181dd517d; and Patricia A. Webster, author reply to Carcillo et al., ibid., 643–644, doi: 10.1097/PCC.0b013e3181e2ea1d.

deemed it "unwarranted and extreme."[52] In defense of that conclusion, they reiterated that DCDD is accepted, established practice that has earned the imprimatur of several national societies and international committees. Consensus and policy statements, they wrote, have emerged to reflect this. Furthermore, they maintained, if certain practitioners are uncomfortable with DCDD protocols, they may be recused from participation. Consequently, a blanket ban on the current protocols would represent a step backward for patient rights. Their heavy emphasis on patient rights reflects the view that individual autonomy should be the overriding consideration, although they slightly repackage that concept by couching the DCDD procedure as an "available care option" the patient has a legal right to choose.

Referring to DCDD, or any type of organ donation, as a form of patient *care* may now be commonplace, but it seems to miss the mark. Care for a patient does not neatly correspond with the act of organ donation, which should properly be considered as a *gift* to another person. It is an extraordinary act on the part of the donor, and any free act of self-giving can be initiated only by the donor or surrogate. Care is something a dying patient receives. An organ is part of oneself that the dying patient actively gives. We do not typically associate the concept of care with an optional surgical procedure

---

52. Thomas A. Nakagawa et al., "A Call for Full Public Disclosure for Donation after Circulatory Determination of Death in Children," *Pediatric Critical Care Medicine* 12.3 (May 2011): 375, doi: 10.1097/PCC.0b013e31820ac30c; and Ari R. Joffe, author reply to Nakagawa et al., ibid., 377–378, doi: 10.1097/PCC.0b013e318216d627.

performed for the benefit of another patient. A healthy, living donor who freely offers one of her kidneys for the sake of another cannot really be said to be the recipient of care, or merely to be selecting from the available care options. The concepts of gift and patient care are neither synonymous nor interchangeable.

Medicare, incidentally, typically pays for approximately 75 percent of transplantations in the United States.[53] Medicare, let us concede, is not an ideal mechanism by which to exchange deep gifts of self. Furthermore, let us suppose that the number of persons with a convicted desire to donate their organs were to exceed the (Medicare) funding available to facilitate all the desired donations. All of those prospective donors would therefore simply be unable to receive the full range of "available care options."

Most other expressions of charity, parenthetically, emanate entirely from the individual who freely decides to be charitable; no intermediaries can stymie these expressions. In the case of organ donation, however, the charitable individual depends not only on a network of skilled physicians, but also on a bureaucratic apparatus with interests of its own. These practical constraints, or even the ultimate ineligibility of a given donor, do not diminish the virtuous intent of any charitably disposed individual, but they may limit its expression. Likewise, any hint of coercion (even if only perceived by the donor) would detract from a freely charitable disposition.

------

53. Tara D. Dixon and Darren J. Malinoski, "Devastating Brain Injuries: Assessment and Management Part I— Overview of Brain Death," *Western Journal of Emergency Medicine* 10.1 (February 2009): 16.

Carcillo and colleagues note that appealing to consensus and patient autonomy sidesteps the central question of whether the donors are actually dead. Autonomy should indeed be respected "to the fullest degree possible," but it is not limitless. They insist that the matter of "whether autonomy alone or in combination with other moral principles can justify violation of the dead donor rule requires open debate."[54] As things stand now, they conclude, truly informed consent does not exist, because these concerns have not been fully disclosed to the public. Several other authors contend likewise.[55]

In similar fashion, Joffe and colleagues argue that DCDD-related consensus statements should not receive undue deference. The issues deserve to be engaged squarely on their merits, yet consensus statements have not adequately done this. Acknowledging the good results that may accrue to recipients, donors, and their families from the practice, the authors hold firm in their belief that "these arguments may be used to make a case

54. Ari R. Joffe, author reply to Nakagawa et al., 378.

55. See, for example, Mohamed Y. Rady, "'Non-heart-beating,' or 'Cardiac Death,' Organ Donation: Why We Should Care," *Journal of Hospital Medicine* 2.5 (September–October 2007): 324, doi: 10.1002/jhm.204. "The interest of organ procurement organizations and affiliates in maximizing recovery of transplantable organs introduces self-serving bias in gaining consent for organ donation and abandons the basic tenet of obtaining true informed consent. The impact of donor management and procurement protocols on end-of-life (EOL) care and the potential trade-off are not disclosed, raising concern about whether potential donors and their families are fully informed before consenting to donation."

for organ donation in the setting of DCD; however, they cannot be used to argue that the donor is dead."[56] Pointing to consensus statements when the death of the donor is not only in doubt, but admittedly not established, appears to be an unsubstantiated appeal to authority.

Carcillo and colleagues also highlight a significant inconsistency worthy of further amplification: the lead authors of the 2006 report of the National Conference on Donation after Cardiac Death, which concluded that DCDD does not violate the dead donor rule, have acknowledged elsewhere that these donors are not ontologically dead. Some physicians, philosophers, and ethicists involved in drafting similar consensus statements have reached the same conclusion independently.[57]

So there is a profound incongruence. Both the consensus statements and the contradictory recognition that some DCDD donors may not be dead can be said to be authoritative. Both, however, do not reflect the physician's specific competency. Since the official consensus statements make judgments that amount to a compromise with respect to biological reality—that DCDD does not *really* amount to violating the dead donor rule, although donors may not be dead even at the five-minute mark—they should be recognized as ethical interpretations of the facts and evaluated on those grounds.

----

56. Joffe et al., "Donation after Cardiocirculatory Death," 1–20.

57. Joffe, author reply to Nakagawa et al., 377.

Benedict XVI's statement on brain death seems to take on even greater urgency in the context of DCDD: "In an area such as this, in fact, there cannot be the slightest suspicion of arbitration and where certainty has not been attained the principle of precaution must prevail."[58] Proceeding with these protocols until more uniformity is achieved seems to conflict with that principle of precaution. Furthermore, there is no guarantee that greater standardization per se will adequately resolve the most important consideration: whether the criterion of irreversibility has been met and the donor may be declared dead with moral certainty. Ultimately, the call for greater standardization is compelling only insofar as the chosen standard is correct and accurate.

This, however, does not necessarily mean that DCDD is never permissible. It does mean that current procedures have to be altered. The first thing would be to institute a more conservative waiting period to establish death with moral certainty, regardless of its effect on organ transplantation. With that proviso in mind, Christopher Kaczor has argued that "the ethical difficulties appear to be surmountable. Properly carried out, DCD is, in my view, ethically permissible even if it remains from a medical point of view technically difficult to successfully perform." This would necessarily entail that sufficient time elapse before death is determined. Kaczor maintains that "even with the demanding

---

58. Benedict XVI, Address to the Pontifical Academy for Life, February 27, 2006.

standard, livers, kidneys, lungs, and perhaps even hearts can be retrieved in cases of DCD."[59]

This, however, would require further intervention to maintain organ viability, since the risk of damage due to warm ischemia rises as time passes. Certain pharmacological agents such as anticoagulants and vasodilators may be administered for that purpose, but there is concern that these agents could hasten the death of the donor. The principle of double effect, however, renders such an intervention morally permissible, alleviating the concern that allowing sufficient time to elapse to ensure death would necessarily result in forfeiting organs.[60]

Kaczor has proposed a solution: once treatment is withdrawn and the foreseeable cardiac arrest ensues, two minutes of asystole should be observed. At that point, ante-mortem interventions may be administered to help preserve the organs, and all other preparations may be made. Only after twenty to thirty minutes have elapsed are the vital organs to be removed.[61] This approach may not always "work," and some types of organs can tolerate delays better than others can. But Kaczor's proposal provides a sound minimum threshold beyond which it would be ethical to proceed, since it satisfies the necessary and sufficient conditions for determining death.

59. Christopher Kaczor, "Philosophy and Theology," column, *National Catholic Bioethics Quarterly* 9.4 (Winter 2009): 781.

60. Eberl, *Thomistic Principles and Bioethics*, 126.

61. Christopher Kaczor, "Organ Donation following Cardiac Death: Conflicts of Interest, Ante Mortem Interventions, and Determinations of Death," in Jensen, *Ethics of Organ Transplantation*, 112.

This does not imply that a formal clinical examination for establishing brain death must be conducted in these circumstances; extending the waiting time would seem to supply sufficient moral certainty of death.

Contentment with the status quo, on the other hand, implies a need to come to terms with a dilution of the dead donor rule. Even proponents of organ donation who reject an ontological interpretation of death (such as Robert Veatch) concede that two minutes of asystole is not enough to satisfy the rule's requirement: the irreversible loss of brain function. Five minutes may well come closer, but Veatch forthrightly asserts that an even longer threshold may be necessary.[62]

The Significance of Finality

The overall conclusions regarding the status of the donor in DCDD protocols may be derived naturally from our understanding of brain death. For some time now, the medical profession has subscribed to a neurocentric view of death: the brain must be irreversibly unable to function for death to occur. The actual determination of brain death must be scrupulous to ensure public confidence, but even if DCDD protocols are always impeccably carried out, confidence that death has actually occurred cannot be ensured. Somewhat paradoxically, this has come to mean that the traditional method of determining death—the loss of cardiopulmonary function—is no longer as straightforward as it seemingly was.

---

62. Robert M. Veatch and Lainie F. Ross, *Defining Death: The Case for Choice* (Washington, DC: Georgetown University Press, 2016), 78.

This is not a simple distinction to convey to the public at large, particularly since the concept of brain death is generally not well understood. The message to be conveyed is that brain death, which many find confusing, is legitimately reliable when rigorously determined, whereas the cessation of heartbeat and respiration, with which many are comfortable, is not satisfactory as currently determined in the context of organ donation. Outside that context, naturally, it still is legitimate. At the very least, prospective donors should be informed that in a DCDD scenario they may not be dead at the time of donation, and that the bedside experience with loved ones will be truncated by the need to move with alacrity.

As currently practiced, DCDD protocols may constitute a form of living donation at least in some cases. While Catholic teaching on organ donation has evolved since the mid-twentieth century, from rejecting to accepting living donation, this approval has always been restricted to particular circumstances; it has never applied to unpaired vital organs or to a complete set of paired vital organs such as the kidneys. For those types of donation, the understanding has always been that the donor must in fact be dead. Benedict XVI strongly reiterated that viewpoint.

Historically, the principle of finality had been the overriding consideration; this principle holds that a person's organs are not meant to be distributed to others, because they are intended (ordered) to carry out their own ends for the sake of that person alone. This implies that living donation would not be permissible. Some theologians argued that it could be justified by appealing to the principle of charity. This justification ultimately carried the day, and living donation is accepted in limited circumstances as long as the donor can maintain functional integrity.

The concept of functional integrity, however, seems inadequate and ambiguous when the donor is clearly in the last moments of life. In this scenario, it would seem that the key question becomes, may an appeal to charity justify organ donation and thereby further erode the principle of finality?

The principle of finality seems to entail that the dead donor rule must require the donor to be dead, not just that the procurement of organs does not constitute an act of direct killing. This seems to be the soundest course of action. Otherwise, there could always be a compelling reason to treat the living person, albeit with some form of consent, in a way that would not be permitted when in the prime of health, however genuinely disposed a patient may be to act with charity.

Siding with finality in this scenario seems to accurately reflect the statements of successive Popes as well as longstanding tradition. It also seems to reasonably maintain the balance between the governing principles that currently allow some forms of living donation but forbid others. Departing from the principle of finality probably would incrementally increase the donor pool; the net effect would be tolerance of the plundering of the body, which John Paul II clearly denounced.

The approval of some forms of living donation that emerged in the twentieth century is often cited as a fine example of the development of doctrine. The uncertain status of the donor in DCDD protocols would seem to require, if not further development per se, further refinement of the relevant principles. Revisiting the underlying basis for why donation is licit in some cases, and reexamining the reasons that death must be established prior to some forms of donation, may help crystalize the most appropriate organ transplantation strategies. Delving into these matters would seem warranted in the current landscape, and any verdict would, in all likelihood, essentially indicate whether charity or finality has the upper hand in these cases.

As your soul departs from your body, may the shining cohort of angels hasten to greet you, the tribunal of apostles acquit you, the triumphant ranks of white-robed martyrs accompany you, the lily-bearing bands of glorious confessors surround you, the choirs of virgins bring up your train with rejoicing, and in blest tranquility may the patriarchs receive you into their loving embrace. May our Lord appear before you gentle and eager of countenance and assign you a place amidst those who stand in his presence for evermore.

—St. Peter Damian

Index